CARPE

M000288194

Tricks of the Trade for
Building & Finishing Your House

Carpentry

Tricks of the Trade for Building & Finishing Your House

BOB SYVANEN

Hartley & Marks
PUBLISHERS

Published by
HARTLEY & MARKS PUBLISHERS INC.

Post Office Box 147	3661 W. Broadway
Pt. Roberts, WA	Vancouver, BC
98281	V6R 2B8

Printed in the U.S.A.

© 1993 (*Carpentry & Exterior Finish*), 1994 (*Carpentry & Interior Finish*), 1996 (*Getting a Good House*)
by The Globe Pequot Press, Inc. a Subsidiary of Morris Communications.
Reprinted with permission of the Globe Pequot Press, Inc., Old Saybrook, CT.

Cover photo of the Bye Residence, Holicong PA, USA
by Jeremiah Eck Architects, Boston, MA
phone: (617) 367-9696
web: www.jearch.com

All rights reserved.
Except for brief reviews, no part of this book may be reproduced in any form or by any means,
electronic or mechanical, including photocopying, recording or by any information storage and retrieval system,
without the written permission of the publisher.

Library of Congress Cataloging-in-Publication Data

Syvanen, Bob, 1928-
      Carpentry : tricks of the trade for building & finishing your
house   /   Bob Syvanen
           p.   cm.
      Includes index.
      ISBN 0-88179-167-9
         1. Carpentry—Miscellanea.   I. Title.
TH5606.S9597   1998
   694—dc21   98-43945
                                                         CIP

Contents

INTERIOR FINISHING

GETTING A GOOD HOUSE

Introduction

The older I get, the more I am convinced that anyone can do anything. All we need is enough desire.

In any endeavor there are the little unforeseen problems that can cause us to stumble; and although there are many how-to books on all manner of subjects, these little unforeseen problems are rarely mentioned. How we deal with these problems is frequently what makes for a success or failure in our efforts.

We read about joists and rafters. We learn where they go, how many nails. But what shall I do when the wood is warped and doesn't do what it is supposed to do? Is there an easy way to pick up lumber and walk with it? Mistakes occur; and although they are not in themselves bad, they do cause us to stumble.

Mistakes are just a different way of doing something—and with a different consequence. Many times a so-called mistake turns out to be the effort with the better consequence. These "mistakes" (of which I have made quite a few) are great learning tools. How we deal with them is what separates the good from the mediocre. When a problem occurs, stay loose; the solution is always there.

I got into carpentry forty years ago because I wanted to be a good architect. I wanted to know about the little problems and their solutions. So for forty years I have been learning to be a carpenter and an architect, and my hope for this book is that it will make at least one job easier for someone.

Remember two things:

1. Measure twice, cut once.

2. You are building a house, not a piano.

Interior Finishing

Lumber Species

Species of lumber can cause problems, but we can overcome. There are five basic choices:

1. Douglas fir
2. Southern or yellow pine
3. Spruce
4. Hemlock
5. Native pine (New England)

DOUGLAS FIR

Number-one choice, along with yellow pine, for framing. When I first started, fir is all I ever saw. It is strong, straight, heavy, and hard. It is highly decay resistant, making it ideal for foundation sills and decks. The problems with fir come from the fact that it is heavy and hard. On some old charts fir was listed as a hardwood. There are five things to be aware of when working with fir:

1. It is heavy.
2. It is hard to cut with a handsaw, particularly a dull handsaw.
3. It is hard to nail.
4. It splits easily.
5. It has bleeding pitch pockets.

Solutions:

1. It's heavy, so get strong.

2. The handsaw is not used as much as in the past, so that presents less of a problem. There are times, however, when it must be used. Make sure it is sharp, and cut with a slow, steady stroke. Be sure the stock is well supported and steady.

3. Good nailing just takes practice and a strong forearm. Before I started my first job, I used to practice nailing every day. I also squeezed a rubber ball to improve my grip.

4. Avoid nailing too close to the end of a board. Don't use a 16d nail when an 8d will do.

5. Bleeding pitch pockets are hard to control. They pose no problem if the lumber is used as a stud or joist; but if it is used as an exposed beam, there could be trouble. Look for a brown spot or streak, especially a crack with the tell-tale brown. Use it with the blemish turned up to keep it from dripping pitch on whatever is below. Sometimes such spots can be cut out and patched, but beware: The pocket can be quite extensive.

SOUTHERN OR YELLOW PINE

Handles like fir but without the pitch pockets. It, too, is heavy, straight, and strong. It also has a lot of resin, which bleeds through paint.

Solution:

Same as for fir. Try different sealers on samples before painting.

SPRUCE

Spruce seems to be the most common framing lumber on the East Coast. It is very light (particularly when dry), easy to cut, and easy to nail, and it sounds wonderful. It does have three weak points:

1. Low decay resistance
2. Poor nail holding
3. Weak

Solutions:

1. Avoid using where moisture is a problem, such as sills and outdoor decks. If it must be used where moisture is present, paint and protect with overhanging or capping sheets of metal. Use pressure-treated lumber for foundation sills.

2. Use adequate nailing, preferably hot-dipped galvanized nails.

3. Use proper sized timber for design loads on building.

HEMLOCK

Hemlock and spruce seem to be what we are offered these days (in New England, at least) for framing. Hemlock, when dry, is quite hard and tends to split. It also twists badly—great if you are making skis. Hemlock has one good quality that I know of. It is a good match for birch and can be used as trim with birch cabinets and doors. It stains similar to birch, but test a few samples first. Hemlock can be recognized by the natural blue streaks in the wood.

Solutions:

1. Use when green, and nail it quick before it gets away.

2. Do not use for outdoor decks.

NATIVE PINE

Native pine of New England is good to work with but getting scarce. Only the small mills cut it. It, too, is highly decay resistant.

CHAPTER TWO

Lumber Finishes and Seasoning

The differences in the species and condition of your lumber can cause problems. There are four condition choices:

1. *Air dry or kiln dry, dressed.* Kiln dry should have less moisture content at the end of the drying process. Air dry takes four months to a year, depending on size. Kiln dry takes one-fourth the time. Both are planed smooth. The mark on the lumber will be "S-Dry" or "Kiln Dry."

2. *Green dressed.* Freshly cut and planed smooth, full of moisture. The mark will be "S-Green."

3. *Green rough cut.* Freshly cut. Rough exterior, full of moisture. No mark; the surface is too rough to take a stamp.

4. *Dry rough cut.* Rough exterior, usually air dry. No marks, too rough. It is very easy, by the weight of the lumber, to tell if it is dry.

Some other marks you will see are "D" for dry and "M.C. 15%" for moisture content 15 percent.

AIR DRY OR KILN DRY, DRESSED

This is the easiest to work with. Mixing air dry and kiln dry causes problems, though, if the air dry has been drying for too short a time. The dimensions of this lumber will be larger than those of the kiln dry, and if you use them together—problems.

Solution:

Use either the kiln dried or the air dried. When using differing dimensioned lumber, you are constantly compensating by shimming up or trimming off (and sometimes forgetting). If using both kiln and air dried, do your compensating act, and use the material where it will matter the least, like rafters.

GREEN DRESSED

Four problems here:

1. It is heavy.
2. Lumber will shrink.
3. Rotting and fungus are encouraged.
4. It does not show pencil mark well.

Solutions:

1. The weight of green lumber can be overcome. Go on a good weight-lifting program. One man can lift one 2" × 10" × 16' green plank; two can be handled if dry.

2. Years ago the framed house dried in the summer sun. It can still be done that way, or a few portable heaters can be used. Practice good fire-prevention methods. Provide ventilation to remove moisture from house as it is driven from the lumber.

3. Separate layers of lumber with sticks as soon as it is delivered. Use 1-inch sticks for thin boards and 2-inch for thick boards.

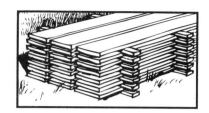

Use an indelible pencil for marking wet lumber, but beware of "blue temple." If you carry the pencil behind the ear, it will leave its mark each time.

DRY ROUGH

The big problem here is the uneven dimensions. A 2 × 4 may measure 2" × 4" at one end and $2\frac{1}{3}$" × $2\frac{1}{4}$" at the other. A 1 × 6 could be $1\frac{1}{2}$" and $\frac{7}{8}$". The larger dimensions vary not only from end to end but also from timber to timber. One may measure $9\frac{3}{4}$"; another, $10\frac{1}{4}$". The better mills have better, but not absolute, control. That is one of the reasons for dressing lumber. It is easier to control the finished size with a planer.

Solution:

Be aware of variations and compensate by shimming and trimming. Use where it matters least.

GREEN ROUGH

Green rough has the same problems as dry rough, with the added bonus of heavy and more shrinkage.

Solution:

Be aware of variations and start a real good weight-lifting program.

CHAPTER THREE

Moving Lumber

All these methods will move lumber, but not without wasting time and energy. None of these show good control, so they are not safe. A man at each end will make easy work of the job, but it will also take twice as long.

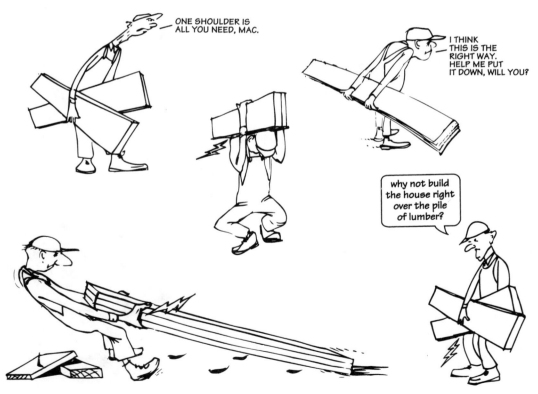

Picking up a single piece of lumber is not a big problem, but forty 2 × 10s are. The best way to carry lumber is on the shoulder, and the quickest is "the lazy man's load," two at a time (twenty trips instead of forty). If the lumber is green, even two might be a bit much to handle. When the load is carried on the shoulder, the sticks must point in the direction you are walking. When carried at waist level, the load is perpendicular to the direction you are walking and the way of the legs. If two boards are carried that way, though, they will scissor.

To pick up a load properly, stand as close to the load as possible with knees bent and back straight. The arms will hang straight at the elbows, with the left hand reaching over to grab the forward edge of the load and the right hand grabbing the rear of the load, thumbs up. With the arms straight and the back kept flat, the powerful leg muscles do the lifting. Don't jerk the load off the ground or the back will bend. Instead, drive hard with the legs; and, as you pass your knees, shrug your shoulders hard. When the load is as high as it will go, drop under it, and at the same time, pivot the body and both feet to the left 90 degrees while rolling the load to catch on the shoulder. The lumber face that was up is now down. To cushion the load as it lands on the shoulder, raise the right arm up and forward. The load will then land on the shoulder muscle instead of the bone. Balance the load by bouncing it off the shoulder and quickly shifting under it. Once the load is balanced, only the right arm, raised and stretched forward on top of the load, is needed for control as you walk.

Back and arms straight . . .

A shrug with the shoulders . . .

Pivot, dip, and onto the right shoulder with right arm raised . . .

The lift is complete ("three white lights," as they say in weight-lifting), and you are on your way.

The load can be tossed from one shoulder to the other by thrusting with the legs. To drop the load either roll it off your shoulder onto your right forearm or toss it up and away with a leg thrust. Practice right and left shoulder with a few light boards.

Moving sheets of plywood or Sheetrock is not one of your fun jobs, but there is a better way than shown here.

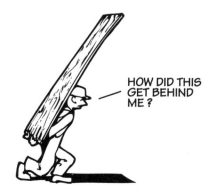

This is awkward. The weight of the sheet is not well distributed, and walking is difficult.

This position is best; the weight is carried on the bottom hand. The top hand keeps the sheet from tipping.

It's a struggle when two people carry one sheet using opposing grips. Each person should have the same carrying hand down (right hand for righties, as shown above).

Lumber Ordering and Stacking

How the lumber is stacked and where it sits on the building site can be great helps in minimizing problems. When making a list for the yard, indicate what the materials are for. Be sure to keep a copy for yourself. The lumber yard will then be able to stack the lumber on the truck in a good sequence. Sometimes yards do a good job and sometimes not. At any rate it should be stacked with the building sequence in mind.

When ordering lumber, don't forget to order at least a half-dozen extra 2" × 10" × 14' planks for scaffolding. Also get two or three bundles of cheap wood shingles for shimming, two dozen 1" × 6" × 16' fence board (an inexpensive board for bracing), and two bundles of 1 × 3 furring strips for bracing.

LUMBER LIST		
EXTERIOR STUDS	2 x 6	400/8'
INTERIOR STUDS	2 x 4	420/8'
FIRST FLOOR JOISTS	2 x 10	50/14'
HEADERS	2 x 10	7/12' 10/14'
SECOND FLOOR JOISTS	2 x 10	50/14'

Before the lumber truck arrives, think about what problems the stack of lumber will cause:

1. Ease of access for truck
2. Ease of unloading
3. Restacking of load
4. Moving lumber from stack to building
5. Location of radial saw and power pole
6. Masonry supplies
7. Traffic flow

Green timber should be stacked crisscrossed and thin boards stacked with 1-inch spacers. Align spacers vertically or thin boards will dry curved. Keep all good lumber off the ground. In the Alpine countries, timber stacks were dried for three years before use. The thin boards were stored for one year.

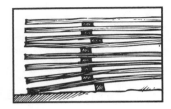

Plywood can be secured by nailing the corners down with 16d nails for half or more of the stack. It helps keep the stack from walking away. Removing nails in the dark is difficult and noisy. Cover with plastic and plenty of wood strips.

Kiln dry lumber should be covered with a tarp; plastic works well. Use plenty of wood strips nailed through the plastic to the stack inside. This cover keeps the rain, snow, and sun off and makes it difficult for this lumber to walk off. I once built a plywood wall around a stack of lumber to keep it from disappearing.

PLOP PLOP PLOP....

Stand rolls of building paper under cover on their ends on a piece of plywood. Rolls that lay on their sides get oval shaped and don't unroll too easily. If they sit on the ground the ends pick up dirt and moisture, again making unrolling difficult.

Columns and Posts

When using temporary posts, cut them about three-quarters of an inch shorter than they should be. It is a simple job to shim up with wood shingles. Use any jacking device available to raise the beam: hydraulic, screw, or auto—even a lever.

It is easier to put the post on the footing with the jack on top. If the jack is on the bottom, the post then has to be balanced on the jack with one hand while you work the jack with the other. Of course with two people, either way will work.

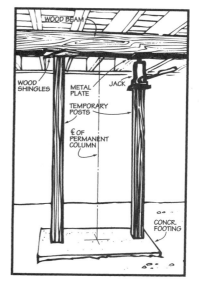

The temporary posts can be secured with a brace each way. Once floor joists are in, the braces can be removed.

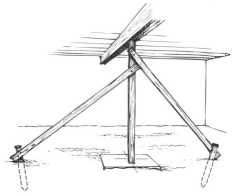

Lally columns are concrete-filled steel tubes. The easiest way to cut them is with a large tubing cutter. Most lumber yards have them and will cut the columns, but you take a chance on their accuracy. The best thing to do is to measure them up, deduct for the top and bottom plates, take them to the yard, and cut them yourself. If they come up a little short, metal shims will bring them up.

You can also cut them on the job with a hacksaw. The ends are always square, so just mark the length four or five places around the column.

Cut most of the way through the metal case all around.

Raise the cut end and rest on a block or another column.

Smack with sledge . . . presto.

CHAPTER SIX

Girders and Beams

When shimming the ends of beams resting on concrete or steel, use a noncompressible material like steel, slate, or asbestos board. Asbestos board works well because it comes in ⅛-inch sheets, which makes it easy to build up, and it cuts easily.

The shims are to keep the beam up permanently, and if wood is used, it will shrink, compress, and maybe even rot away. Plywood works pretty well; its compression loss is minimal.

SHIM BELOW BEAM

Sills

Sills are the most important step in the building. If all is square and level, then the rest will go quite easily.

STEPS FOR SETTING SILLS

1. Establish true and square corners.
2. Establish the inside corners of sills.
3. Mark inside edge of sills.
4. Select material for sills.
5. Locate anchor bolt holes on sill; drill.
6. Set sills in place.
7. Level sills.
8. Install termite barrier.

ESTABLISHING TRUE AND SQUARE CORNERS

After the foundation has been completed, check its length and width against the plan. If sides are equal and diagonals are equal, then the foundation is square. If not, an adjustment must be made.

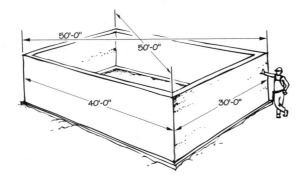

50'-0"
50'-0"
40'-0"
30'-0"

The exact diagonal can be found mathematically ($a^2 + b^2 = c^2$); and with small pocket calculators, it is easy. There are special slide rules that give the diagonal with a twist of a dial. Just keep adjusting corners until you hit the dimensions required.

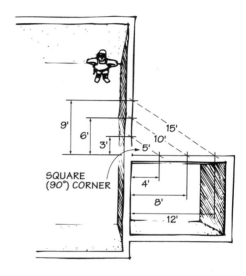

If you have a foundation that is more than a simple rectangle, the 3, 4, 5 triangle is very helpful. After the main foundation is squared, an addition can be squared off any wall with the 3, 4, 5 triangle. The 3, 4, 5 triangle is the same as $a^2 + b^2 = c^2$ ($3^2 + 4^2 = 5^2$).

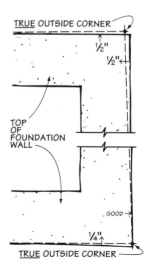

When the corners are established, mark them on the foundation. If a corner is ½ inch outside of the concrete, mark ½" ↑. If it is ½ inch in on the concrete, mark ½" ←. If an edge is right on, mark "good."

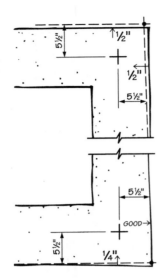

TRUE INSIDE CORNER

Take a short block of the sill material and place it at the corner, the true outside corner. Mark the inside face on the foundation. Use a nail to scratch a good mark each way forming a "+" for the true inside corner.

MARK INSIDE EDGE OF SILLS

With corners marked, snap a red chalk line connecting the inside corners. This is the inside edge of the sill; use it for control. It doesn't matter what the foundation does. Red chalk shows up better on concrete, but blue will do.

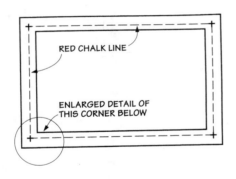

MATERIAL FOR SILLS

The best is pressure treated; and, in fact, many areas of the country require its use.

Douglas fir is the next choice because of its high decay resistance. Any other wood is all right if moisture is kept away. Choose straight pieces.

LOCATE ANCHOR BOLTS

Rest the sill on the foundation alongside bolts at its
proper location relative to the true outside corner.
With a combination square, locate and mark the
center line of bolts.

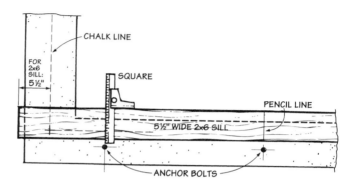

Measure from center line of bolts to chalk line,
transfer to sill. Drill $^7/_8$-inch hole for $^1/_2$-inch bolt
to allow for adjusting.

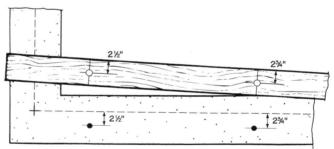

There are usually a few anchor bolts leaning . . .

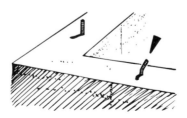

To straighten, beat them over with a hand maul, but screw a nut on and hit it instead of the bolt threads.

Locating anchor-bolt holes is easy with this tool. Align the outside face of the sill with the chalk line. With the tool in place, hammering on the self-tapping screw locates the bolt hole.

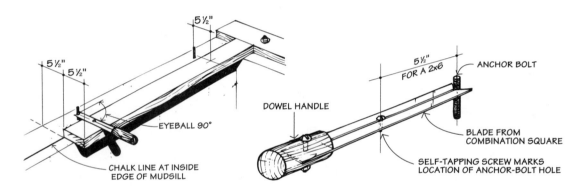

5½"

5½" 5½"

——EYEBALL 90°

DOWEL HANDLE

5½"
FOR A 2x6

ANCHOR BOLT

BLADE FROM
COMBINATION SQUARE

SELF-TAPPING SCREW MARKS
LOCATION OF ANCHOR-BOLT HOLE

CHALK LINE AT INSIDE
EDGE OF MUDSILL

INSTALLING SILLS

Lightly bolt the first corner sill piece in place, lining up with the inside corner chalk line and the true outside corner. The next piece is then butted up against it, and the same procedure is followed for bolt locations. When all the sill pieces are in place, recheck lengths, widths, and diagonals. Adjust if necessary.

LEVELING SILLS

The most accurate tool for leveling is the water tube level. It is just a long piece of clear plastic tubing with a colored antifreeze solution in it. There are garden hose attachments available, but the problem with a garden hose is that you can't see if the line is clear of bubbles. The line must be clear or you will not get a true reading.

Using the tube is very simple. Keep one end at the high point of the foundation and move the other to various points around the wall. The water will seek the same level at each end, and you can note the variations in wall heights. Mark these height differences on the wall: +½", −¼", and so on.

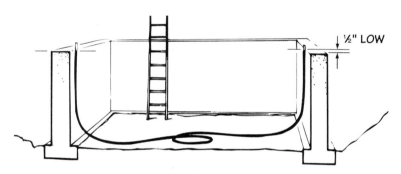

½" LOW

The builder's level is good as long as care is taken when setting up. Try to keep the "shots" short. The further away from the instrument, the greater the error.

INSTRUMENT OUT OF LEVEL

SIGHT LINE

LEVEL LINE

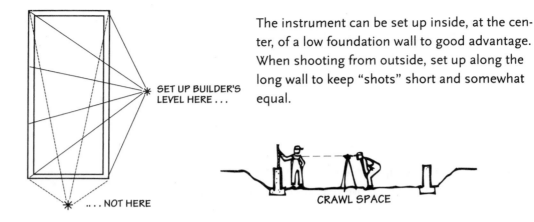

SET UP BUILDER'S
LEVEL HERE . . .

. . . NOT HERE

CRAWL SPACE

The instrument can be set up inside, at the center, of a low foundation wall to good advantage. When shooting from outside, set up along the long wall to keep "shots" short and somewhat equal.

Set up a reference point that you can check easily. Someone is bound to kick one of the tripod legs. You can use a nail in a tree or some stationary object, a ruler, or a wood soldier.

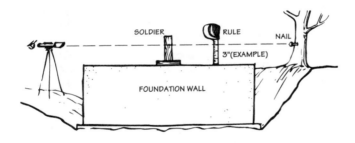

SOLDIER   RULE   NAIL

3"(EXAMPLE)

FOUNDATION WALL

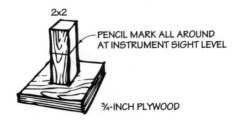

2x2

PENCIL MARK ALL AROUND AT INSTRUMENT SIGHT LEVEL

¾-INCH PLYWOOD

As long as the cross hairs hit the original reference mark (nail in tree, mark on ruler, mark on wood soldier), all is well. If the instrument is moved, a new reference point must be established. Keep checking. There is an old carpenter's saying: "Measure twice, cut once."

Steps in leveling sills:

1. Locate high point.
2. Take reading on ruler.
3. Take reading at each bolt and add ½ inch for grout.
4. Cut wood shim of thickness required at each bolt.
5. Paint cement wash on foundation top to aid bonding of grout.
6. Put mortar bed in place.
7. Put sills on.
8. Finish exposed edges of mortar bed.

1. With sills in place, locate the high point, making sure sill is in contact with foundation.

2. & 3. Take a reading on a ruler and add ½ inch for mortar bed. The bed serves two purposes: A good seal and good support. Do the same at each bolt, making sure ½ inch is added. Record dimensions on sill.

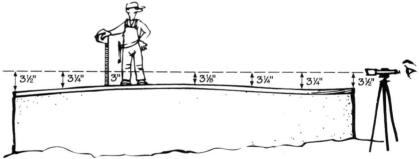

4. Cut shims, 2 inches by 2 inches by thickness required at each bolt.

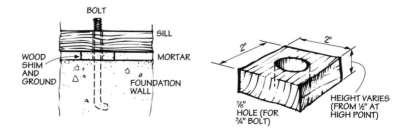

5. Paint top of foundation with a thin creamy paste of cement and water.

6. & 7. Mix a rich batch of mortar and apply to top of foundation wall. Keep it soft so that the sill will have no trouble compressing it to the level of the shims. Keep the mortar away from shims to make sure it does not ooze over on top, preventing the sill from sitting on the shims.

←MORTAR BED→

TOP OF FOUNDATION WALL

If sill piece is warped, that is, has a bow in it, put the hump up and press it into the mortar with a strong straight edge.

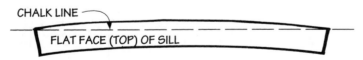

If sill piece has a "crook," sometimes called a "crown" or "wow," it can be used if you snap a chalk line and cut it straight.

CHALK LINE

FLAT FACE (TOP) OF SILL

8. Clean up squeezed-out mortar, and smooth with trowel.

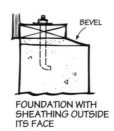

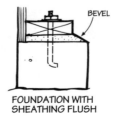

FOUNDATION WITH SHEATHING OUTSIDE ITS FACE

FOUNDATION WITH SHEATHING FLUSH

FOUNDATION WITH EXTERIOR INSULATION

BEVEL

BEVEL

BEVEL IF NO TERMITE BARRIER

Grouting the mudsill after it is installed allows the framing to progress. The grouting can then be done at any time; however, there should be easy access to both sides of the sill.

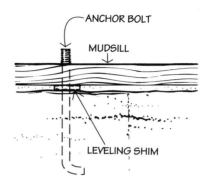

Install wood-shim spacers to bring the sill to the proper level (allowing ½ inch minimum grouting).

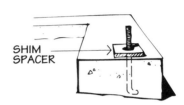

Install mudsill, joists, and headers. Shim mudsill up to joist header where necessary by using narrow strips of wood shingles.

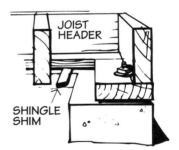

Grout under mudsill by throwing mortar into the space between mudsill and foundation. Push mortar to center with shingle butt. Fill all space under mudsill.

TERMITE BARRIER

Where termites are a problem, a barrier is a must. The best material is 20-ounce copper. Zinc and aluminum will work. Silica-gel, a drying agent, has been used experimentally as a permanent termite control sprinkled around a building during construction. It is extremely absorbent, and when it touches an insect's shell, it eats a hole in it and then goes on to dehydrate the critter. Because insects have exoskeletons, they are the only ones affected by silica-gel. It is totally nontoxic to folks and other animals. I know it works on fleas in a house. It is used to dry flowers, and is used in packaging and in refrigeration.

This termite barrier is the best choice where infestation is bad. It offers the best protection but is the most costly.

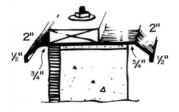 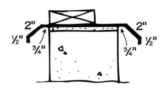

This termite barrier is good for most conditions.

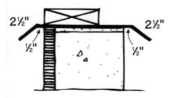 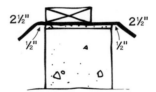

This termite deflector is good where infestation is not too bad. It is the least expensive. Use only when top of foundation is easily visible, such as basement areas. Do not use with crawl spaces.

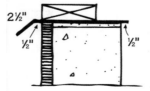 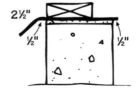

BENDING SHEET METAL

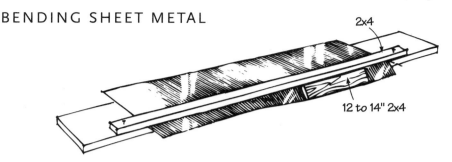

Beating on sheet metal with a hammer doesn't make for a neat bend. Setting up like a sheet-metal shop's "brake" helps do a neat job, and it is quicker.

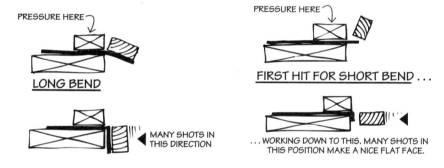

Use pieces of whatever length you can handle. Shorter is easier, only it means more seams. Locate the anchor-bolt holes, drill, and put the first piece in place. Lap the next piece (1 inch for copper, 1½ inches for zinc or aluminum), locate bolts, drill, and place on foundation. At corners, lap 1 inch for copper and full lap for zinc or aluminum. When all pieces are in place, clean joints and solder just like copper tubing. If zinc or aluminum is used, a lock seam should be used.

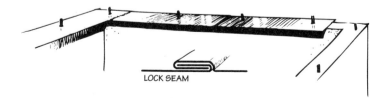

To bend a termite barrier in place, use a block of the required thickness to bend the metal over. It is a good two-man job, but not impossible for one. Always put pressure on a block of wood on top of the sheet to keep it from bulging up. Make bends by beating with a block of wood.

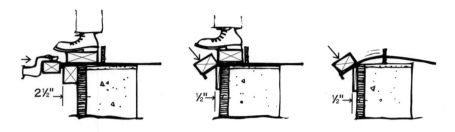

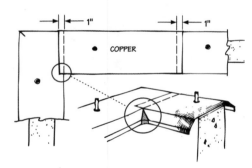

With copper, inside corners are cut, filled with a wedge, and soldered.

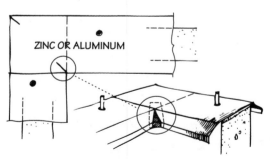

With zinc or aluminum, inside corners are cut and the resulting gap filled with a rectangle slipped under and caulked.

Beam pockets should be fully lined.

Joists and Headers

There are basically two types of framing: "balloon framing," and "platform or Western framing." The exterior wall studs in platform framing are broken at each floor by joists and headers. The studs in the balloon framing are unbroken, with the joists resting on the sill at foundation level and on ledger strips at the other floor levels. The balloon framing is ideal for the energy-conserving house. The exterior walls have unbroken insulation, between the studs, from roof to foundation.

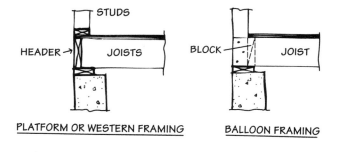

PLATFORM OR WESTERN FRAMING   BALLOON FRAMING

An ideal combination is balloon framing with the superinsulated walls. If properly built, superinsulated houses need very little heating other than sunlight through windows, the heat of appliances, lights, and body heat.

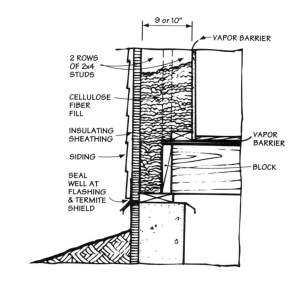

Mark an "X" on the crown edge, preferably on each end so you won't have to hunt for it. Use a soft-lead pencil, lumber crayon, or felt-tip pen.

Check the ends for square, both ends if you need them.

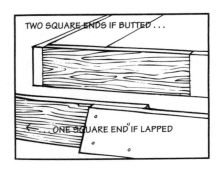

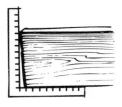

Always measure from a squared end.

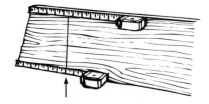

Watch out for pieces of wood or dirt hanging on the end, especially when using a tape measure that hooks over the end.

With the sills square and level, the joist and headers should go in easily. Use straight pieces for headers. If one has a slight crown, it can be pulled down with toenailing.

Start with the header a little outside the sill so that when it is driven home, it will be flush. When toenailing, always hit the nail, not the wood. Let the nail do the pulling.

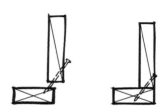

If the header still doesn't line up when the nail is driven home, use another toenail. Really pound those nails. If necessary use three, not too close together; the wood might split.

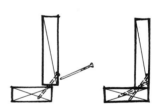

Joists should be laid in crown up. The weight of the floor will flatten them out in time. If joists are chosen randomly, there will be high joists next to low joists, making for a very uneven floor.

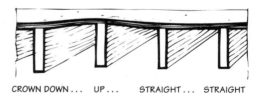

CROWN DOWN . . .   UP . . .   STRAIGHT . . . STRAIGHT

To find the crown, sight down the length of the "stick" while it is lying on the pile. If you pick up one end, it will sag making a curved sight line.

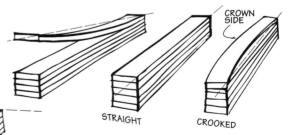

CROWN SIDE

STRAIGHT   CROOKED

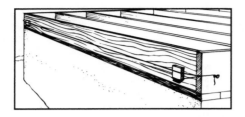

Each end joist should be straightened. The best way to see if an end joist is straight is to stretch a string (Mason's line) from one end to the other over 3/4-inch shim blocks at each end. The reason for the shim blocks is to make sure the string does not touch the joist. Slip another 3/4-inch block between string and joist, at various points along the joist, and you will see how much out or in it is.

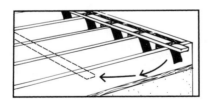

Straighten joist and hold in place with a diagonal brace. Sitting down and pushing with the powerful leg muscles will make any stubborn joist move. Leave the nail heads up for easy removal.

With the header and end joists straight and securely braced, the rest of the joists can be straightened. Take 1 × 3 furring strips and mark off the joist spacings at the header. Then move the stick 5 or 6 feet away from the header and tack each joist in its proper place. Make sure the strip is at least 50 inches back from the header to allow for one row of plywood. Stay clear of the bridging.

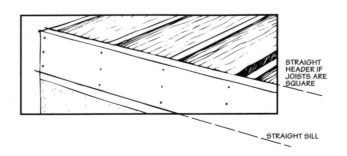

STRAIGHT HEADER IF JOISTS ARE SQUARE

STRAIGHT SILL

If the sill is straight, then the header will be straight on the bottom; if the joists are square, then the header will be straight on the top.

If joists are not square but instead tip in or out, the header will not be straight on top.

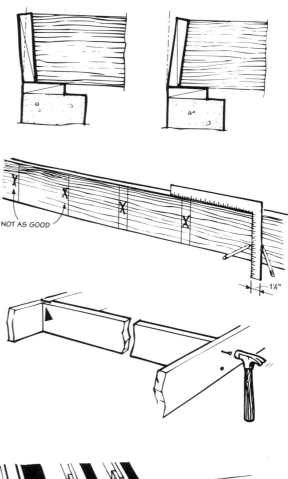

When marking joist locations on a header, a single line with an "X" on the side against which the joist is to go will do, but many mistakes are made here. The joist is often put on the wrong side. Better to mark both sides of the joist and put an "X" in the middle.

For joist installation by one person, a folded-over nail supplies support at one end while you nail at the other.

I've put in 12-foot pressure-treated 2 × 8s using this system.

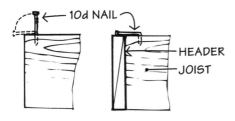

Setting joists to a snapped chalk line on the mudsill makes for a straight header and easy installation.

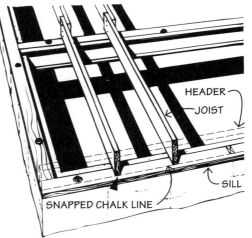

CHAPTER NINE

Bridging

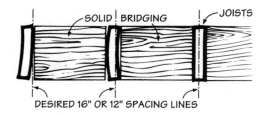

Solid bridging has a few problems that make it bothersome to put in. It tends to creep or gain if there are problem joists. This requires attention and adjusting. Plumbers don't like this type of bridging (more holes to drill). Most of the time they just knock any block out that gets in the way.

Although the mathematical size of the blocking is 14½ inches (for joists 16 inches on center) or 10½ inches (for joists 12 inches on center), cut them a tad short, about 1/16 inch. And test a few in place. Keep eyeballing down the joists to make sure they are not bowing.

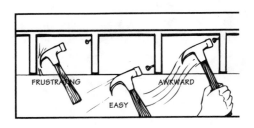

Bridging should not be nailed solid until the building is complete. This allows all the joists to equalize and settle. With solid bridging it is not easy to drive home the top nail after the deck is in place. It is tough enough with a 2 × 8 at 16 inches on center; imagine a 2 × 12 at 12 inches on center. You have to swing the hammer in an arc and, at the right time (trial and error), go for the nail.

If Sheetrock is to go on the ceiling below with no furring strips (strapping in New England) over the joists, then the blocking must be put in with care. They must not hang below joist bottoms. Chop bottoms off those that do with a hatchet.

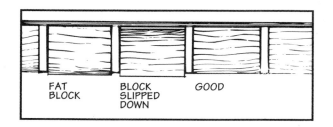

Prenail the joist for solid bridging. The top nail is nailed when you are standing on a plank alongside the chalk line marking the center line of the blocking. The blocks are staggered, so stagger the nails. The bottom nails are best nailed from below. Load the plank with blocks and nail them in place with the top nail only. Drive it home hard to pull the block against the joist. The bottom nail is driven home from below when all blocks are in place.

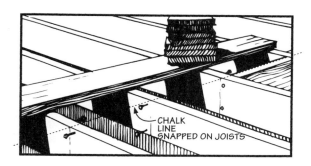

DIAGONAL WOOD BRIDGING

1 × 3 or 1 × 4 wood bridging can be obtained precut at most lumber yards. Cutting it on the job is not too difficult once you set up a jig. The easiest tool for the job is the radial saw, but a Skil-Saw and miter box setup works fine. The simplest way to find the size is to draw it on a piece of scrap joist material.

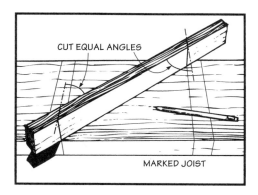

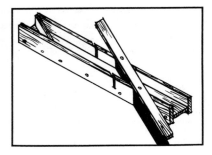

With the angle and length of the bridging known, you can set up a miter box. If the angle is less than 45 degrees, the bridging will have to be cut vertically because a Skil-Saw will not adjust to less than 45 degrees. 1 × 4 bridging will need a 9-inch Skil-Saw to reach the full depth.

Narrow bays (less than 16 inches on center or 12 inches on center) will have to be cut with a handsaw. Either draw it on a piece of scrap or mark it in place.

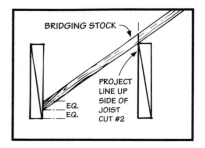

BRIDGING STOCK
PROJECT LINE UP SIDE OF JOIST CUT #2
EQ.
EQ.

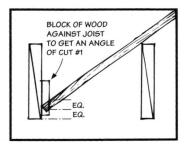

BLOCK OF WOOD AGAINST JOIST TO GET AN ANGLE OF CUT #1
EQ.
EQ.

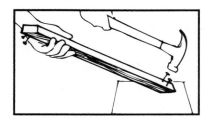

Prenail the bridging with two nails on top and two nails on the bottom.

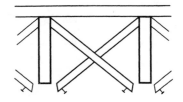

Lay a plank on the joist alongside the chalk line, marking the center line of the bridging. Load up the plank with the prenailed bridging. Nail the top end only.

Keep the bottoms of the bridging up a tad from the bottom of the joist for better bearing.

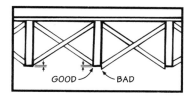

Sometimes there is a problem driving in a block at an angle into a tight place. The top corner digs in and won't move. Beat on this corner with a hammer to round it off. It should at least start easier, but if it still won't go, beat on the corner diagonally opposite.

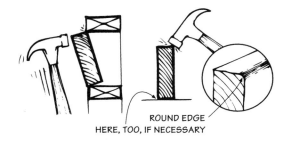

Decking

PLYWOOD

Eyeball down the joists to check for straightness. You can pick up errors quickly that way.

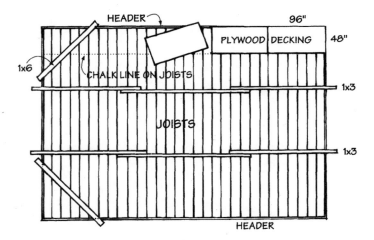

Because of today's poor quality control, the plywood sheets should be checked for size. They can be as much as ⅛ inch longer and wider than 48 inches × 96 inches. Combined with the 6d-nail spacing (required) between sheets, this error makes for quite a gain at the end of four sheets. If you don't compensate by gaining a little on the joist spacing, you will have to cut plywood sheets so that they hit halfway on a joist.

Snap a chalk line on top of the joists at 48 inches from the header and lay the plywood sheets to that line. The header may be straight, but the chalk line is straighter. Put a few sheets to walk on, but be sure the ends are supported. Tack the first row in place, leaving the nail heads up for easy removal. Put one nail in each corner to keep the sheets flat. Proceed with a few more rows, tacking and spacing. The reason for tacking is that, no matter how careful you are, the sheets will have to be adjusted to come halfway on a joist. When a few rows have been adjusted and set, drive the "tacked" nails home. This gets rid of the little toe trippers. Lay the rest of the sheets in place, adjust, and tack. Snap chalk lines across the deck on joist center lines. Nail it up.

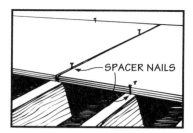

Adjust plywood sheets by jumping up and in the direction the sheet should go. As you land, drive your feet in the direction of movement. Vary intensity of movement by varying effort. The smaller the effort, the less the movement.

Big effort, big movement . . .

After the deck is on and nailed, it can be easily checked for level with a builder's level (transit) and a wood soldier. It is a good time to set Lally columns, too.

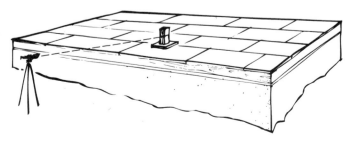

T&G DECKING

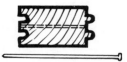

T&G decking comes in 1-, 2-, 3-, and 4-inch thicknesses (³/₄, 1½, 2½, and 3½ inches). Try to buy from a good mill or be prepared to struggle getting the pieces together. The 3- and 4-inch types are produced only by the bigger mills. They are also double tongued, so they had better fit well. They are predrilled for large spikes. A heavy hammer or a light maul is a must.

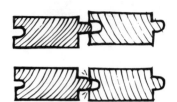

A poor fit is the result of poor milling. The tongue is usually slightly larger than the groove. Sometimes it's the alignment that is out.

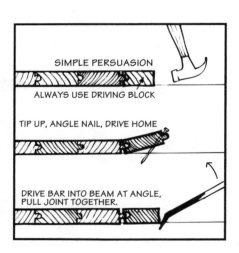

SIMPLE PERSUASION

ALWAYS USE DRIVING BLOCK

TIP UP, ANGLE NAIL, DRIVE HOME

DRIVE BAR INTO BEAM AT ANGLE, PULL JOINT TOGETHER.

Even with the variations involved, all will go together with the proper persuasion. A heavy hammer, prybars, toe nails, and a few tricks will help. If the piece is bowed badly, two prybars can be used alternately to walk the stick in. A combination of any or all can be used.

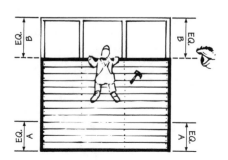

EQ. B   EQ. B

EQ. A   EQ. A

Keep checking the ends for gain and straightness. Begin measuring from the starting edge to the last board laid. Eyeball down the length for straightness. When past the middle, switch to measuring to the finishing edge.

Gap the weak end to gain a little with each new row. Make sure strong end gets driven home.

If the middle is bowing out, drive it hard and gap the edges. If a constant check is made, the corrections will be minor. A 2-inch surprise with three boards left is not easy to make up.

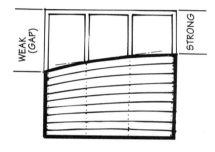

CHAPTER ELEVEN

Exterior Walls

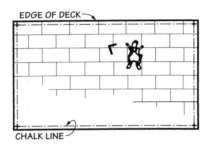

EDGE OF DECK

CHALK LINE

Even though the sill was squared, another check is in order here. Establish the true outside corners and mark the true inside corners using a block of whatever the exterior wall plate is (2 × 4, 2 × 6 . . .). The deck, like the foundation, cannot be changed; so the corners are altered as were the sills. Snap a chalk line connecting the corners, establishing the inside edge of the exterior walls. The walls go to this line regardless of what the deck does. If the sill and joist were done with care, the outside face of the exterior wall should line up pretty well with the outside face of the deck.

The exterior walls are built on the deck, covered with plywood, then tipped up into position. If anything other than plywood is used, diagonal let-in braces must go in each corner.

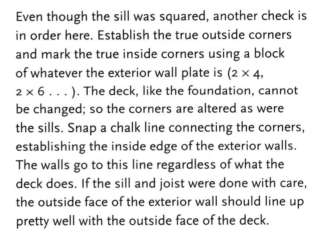

STOP - (2) 2x4s
NAILED TO DECK

90°

2x4s BELOW
KEEP SAW
BLADE
CLEAR OF
DECK

2x4s TO BE CUT

SAW GUIDE

SAW SHOE TO
BLADE DIMENSION

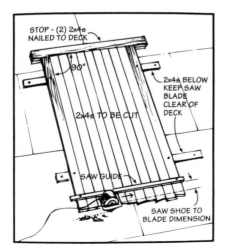

Most lumber yards will precut studs. They cost more but are worth it. A radial-arm saw on the job does just what the lumber yard does. A power saw with a jig setup on the deck works well not only for studs but also for other multiple cuts. Here is a good time for "measure twice, cut once." I ignored it one time and cut all the exterior studs 12 inches short.

I overcame that error by building a 12-inch wall, using it as the windowsill height and then putting the short stud wall on it.

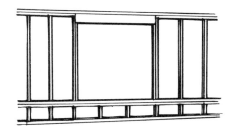

My short-stud-wall error made me aware of the problems in using a tape measure. It is an ideal tool for a left-handed person because the tape is held in the right hand and the pencil in the left. The tape is then naturally hooked to the left end of the board, extended to the right and read left to right.

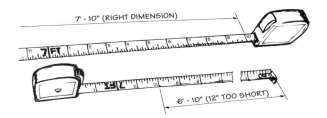

A righty holds the tape in the left hand, pencil in the right. The natural motion is to hook the tape on the right end of the board and then extend the tape to the left. A righty must then read the unnatural way, right to left. If the tape is hooked on the left end, the righty has to turn the hand over, extend to the right, and cross over with the right hand to mark, all of which is very awkward. This backward reading causes many errors. Six and one-half inches will be read short by going first to the full number and then to the *right* ½ inch for a reading of 5½ inches.

Cut top and bottom plates in pairs.

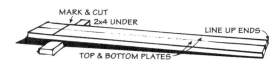

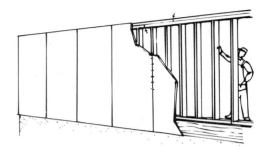

The top and bottom plates do not have to be on a 48-inch module to accommodate plywood. They can be butted anywhere because the double top plate and the lapped plywood will tie them together.

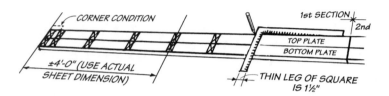

Mark stud locations on upper and lower plates for the entire wall. To do this, butt all plates together.

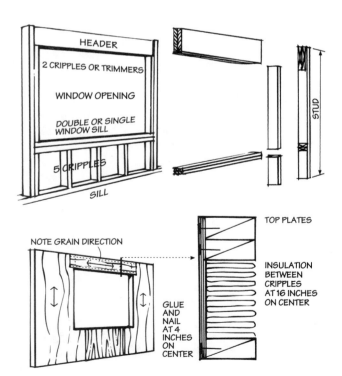

Cut sills, headers, trimmers, and cripples for all windows and doors. Code mark and set aside for use as needed. If a radial saw is not available for this, use the jig setup for stud cutting and adjust for the lengths required. To get accurate dimensions for the pieces, draw the locations of the sill and header on a stud. Use blocks of header and sill material. A 2 × 10 header could measure $9\frac{1}{4}$ inches to $9\frac{1}{2}$ inches. Two 2 × 4s should measure 3 inches, but not always. When stacked together, these gains multiply. After cutting one set, check it on the stud.

A header does not have to be spaced. Pack out with ½-inch drywall inside.

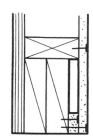

A good header for an energy-efficient house is an insulated box beam.

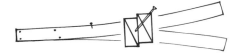

If two 2 × 4s have to be nailed together, it is a good opportunity to use up the crooked ones by opposing the bends. Start at one end and work up the board to the other, toenailing as you go.

Snap a line parallel to the deck edge for the length of the building. Nail 2 × 4 blocks, for stops, on this line. The top plate will be built to these blocks. Three blocks on the edge of the deck will hold the wall square while assembling.

The entire wall is built on the deck. Check the diagonals of the complete wall; they should be equal. Toenail the bottom plate to the deck, driving the top plate hard against the blocks. Leave the nail heads out for easy removal. If sheathing other than plywood is used, let-in diagonal bracing must be used. This is explained in Chapter 12, Interior Partitions.

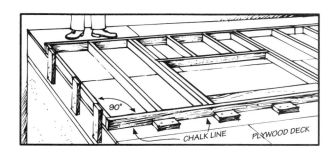

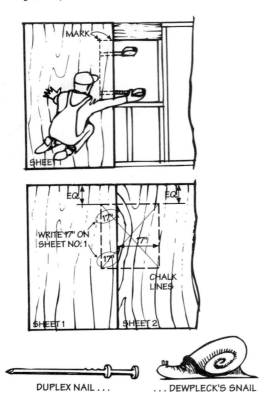

Butt the plywood tight, one piece to another. There is no problem of swelling from moisture here, but each section should be gapped to make sure the plates come tight and no wall gain occurs. Be careful not to nail the plates where the plywood overlaps (you can't raise the entire wall in one piece). Window and door openings are marked on the plywood as it goes on. A power saw makes quick work of cutting them out while the wall is still flat on the deck.

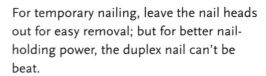

DUPLEX NAIL . . .   . . . DEWPLECK'S SNAIL

For temporary nailing, leave the nail heads out for easy removal; but for better nail-holding power, the duplex nail can't be beat.

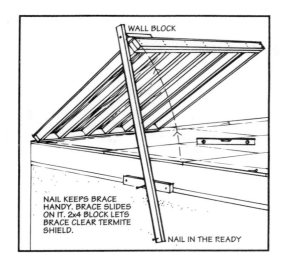

NAIL KEEPS BRACE HANDY. BRACE SLIDES ON IT. 2x4 BLOCK LETS BRACE CLEAR TERMITE SHIELD.

When the first section of wall is raised, it will have to have a temporary brace. The brace must not interfere with the wall that goes at right angles with it in the corner. A 2 × 4 spacer block is nailed to the sill below, and a 2 × 4 block is nailed to the top of the partition. To these blocks the temporary brace is nailed. Nail the 1 × 3 brace to the wall block and put a nail at the ready in the other end. A nail for the brace to slide on is a great help. Raise the wall section, drive it into position with a sledge, rough plumb, and nail the brace. Before raising the wall, check the bottom plate for

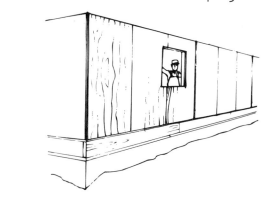

nails or pebbles stuck to it. Tack the bottom plate with a few nails, leaving an option to move it. The other sections follow.

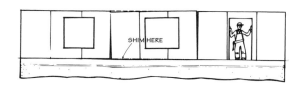

Brace the middle sections through the window openings. A diagonal brace nailed to a 2 × 4 block nailed through the deck into a joist will do. If the sections don't line up because of a dip in the deck, shim them with wood-shingle tips to bring in line.

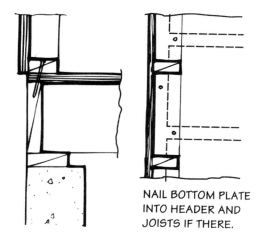

Secure sections together when they are adjusted in place and braced back to the deck, allowing room for building the adjacent walls. Build the adjacent walls the same way. Raise the corner section, drive into position, and tack the bottom plate. The corner is pulled together and tacked. Check for plumb each way. It should be on the money if the panels are square and the deck is level. Once all the walls are in place, the bottom plate should be nailed securely. Make sure to hit the joist and header below.

NAIL BOTTOM PLATE INTO HEADER AND JOISTS IF THERE.

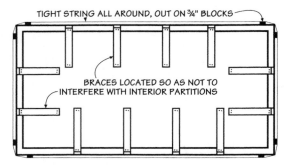

TIGHT STRING ALL AROUND, OUT ON ¾" BLOCKS

BRACES LOCATED SO AS NOT TO INTERFERE WITH INTERIOR PARTITIONS

PLAN AT TOP OF WALL

The exterior walls are now checked for square with the diagonal measurements. Adjustments are best made with a "come along" winch pulling the long diagonal. Finish all the loose ends, and nail loose and missing plywood. It is more efficient if done now and less likely to be forgotten. The walls are straightened with spring braces. Shimmed strings around the perimeter are the guide lines.

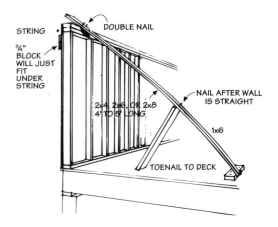

STRING

¾" BLOCK WILL JUST FIT UNDER STRING

DOUBLE NAIL

2x4, 2x6, OR 2x8 4' TO 5' LONG

NAIL AFTER WALL IS STRAIGHT

1x6

TOENAIL TO DECK

A spring brace is a 1" × 6" × 16' board nailed to the top plate of a wall to be straightened, and to the deck as well. The wall is pulled in by pushing up or bowing the middle of the brace with a 50-inch length of 2 × 4.

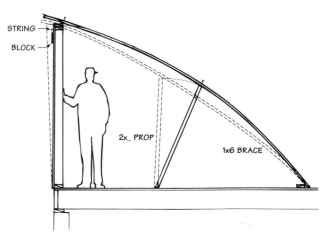

STRING

BLOCK

2x_ PROP

1x6 BRACE

Very fine control can be achieved this way, even by one person. Bow the brace, tack in place, and check the string for ³/₄-inch clearance. The braces have to be checked, as each new one that goes in affects the others. Leave the strings up for periodic checking, but make sure the ³/₄-inch shims are in at each end.

Toenail the bottom plate to the deck to keep the partition from sliding when it is raised.

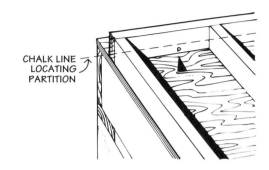

CHALK LINE LOCATING PARTITION

For spring braces to work properly, the bottom anchor block must be nailed to a pair of joists.

The bottom of the spring brace should be clear of the deck.

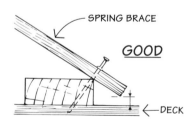

SPRING BRACE

GOOD

←DECK

Adjusting the spring brace when the bottom is too close to the deck pulls the nails and loosens the spring brace.

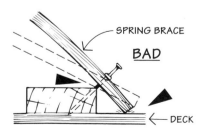

SPRING BRACE

BAD

←DECK

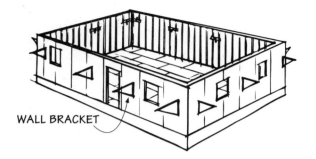

WALL BRACKET

If exterior wall brackets are used, they all go on after the exterior walls are secured straight. The holes in the sheathing for these brackets are drilled in the first stud bay in each corner and spaced to accommodate the staging planks.

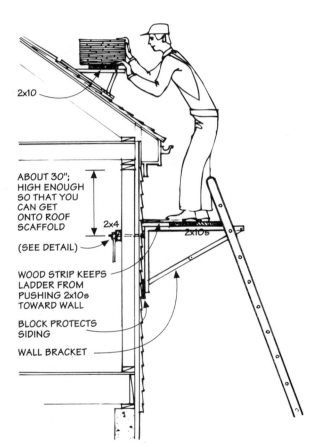

2x10

ABOUT 30"; HIGH ENOUGH SO THAT YOU CAN GET ONTO ROOF SCAFFOLD

2x4

(SEE DETAIL)

WOOD STRIP KEEPS LADDER FROM PUSHING 2x10s TOWARD WALL

2x10s

BLOCK PROTECTS SIDING

WALL BRACKET

The holes are 30 inches down from the top plate. Staging planks should be no longer than 14 feet. Twelve-foot planks are more comfortable, less bouncy. Drill holes large enough so there is no struggle to get the bracket shaft through. Nail a 1 × 3 kicker stick on top of the planks so that it reaches over to the siding. This will keep the planks from being pushed in by a heavy ladder load leaning against them. Put a stick wherever a ladder will go. Nail a 1-inch by 3-inch by 18-inch cleat across both planks at the midpoint. It makes the two planks one.

NAIL

2x4

2x4 BLOCK

BLOCK PREVENTS SCAFFOLD FROM BREAKING 2x4 CROSS PIECE; NAIL PREVENTS 2x4 FROM SLIPPING OFF STUDS

CHAPTER TWELVE

Interior Partitions

If there is to be no plywood deck on the second floor, the exterior walls will have to be permanently stabilized. (The spring braces are only temporary.) The best way to do this is with a 1" by 3" diagonal let-in brace in a perpendicular butting partition. If there is a second floor deck, these partitions can be secured with temporary braces.

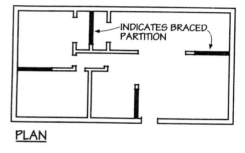

INDICATES BRACED PARTITION

PLAN

Build partitions on the deck with let-in braces just tacked in place at the top and bottom plates. Make sure each partition is square and secure before cutting notches for the 1" by 3" diagonal brace. Raise partition into place and secure to exterior wall before double nailing brace to top and bottom plate and each stud. If brace is not let in, and not permanent, tack a diagonal brace on the surface of the partition.

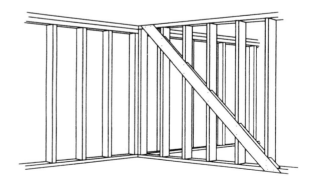

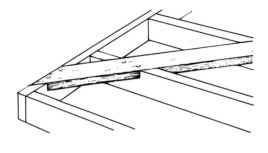

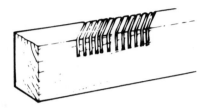

To cut notches, use a power saw set for a $3/4$-inch-deep cut. With partition square and secure on the deck, tack a guide strip diagonally on partition and cut. Move the guide strip over so that the saw will cut the width of the brace; then cut. Cut in between these two parallel cuts, spacing cuts $1/16$-inch to $1/8$-inch apart.

It will be easy to break away these thin pieces with a hammer. Clean out bottom of notch with a sharp chisel.

If the standard framing requiring three studs, or blocking and a nailer, at partition intersections is used, a bowed end stud is desirable.

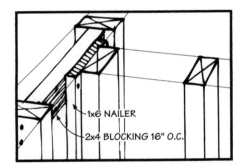

1x6 NAILER

2x4 BLOCKING 16" O.C.

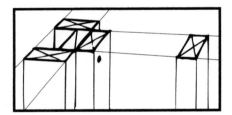

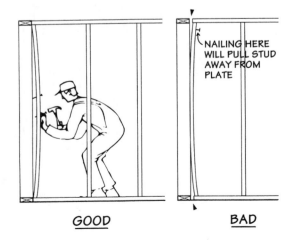

NAILING HERE WILL PULL STUD AWAY FROM PLATE

GOOD   BAD

The bowed condition forces the top and bottom plates to be pulled tight against the adjoining partition. Also keep the end stud a tad back from the end of the top and bottom plates.

If drywall corner clips or plywood plates (a floating corner) are used, then a straight stud is a must. This floating corner at an exterior wall intersection is ideal for the energy-efficient house because of its better insulating qualities.

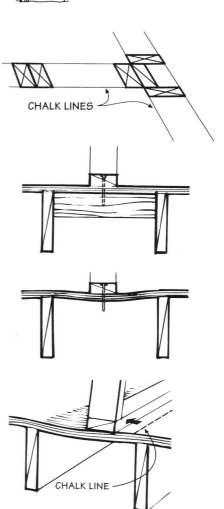

Interior partitions are laid out with chalk lines on the deck. Snap a line for each side of the partition (no guessing where the partition goes that way). Pencil anything that should show up easily and should last.

Nail bottom plate to solid wood below, whether joists or blocking.

Plywood alone will sag . . .

. . . and partition moves off chalk line too easily.

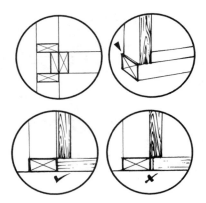

When one partition intersects another, be sure the end stud is kept back a tad from the end of the top and bottom plates. If it is too strong on the plates, the partition will not come up tight. This is a simple step that takes no extra time.

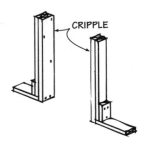

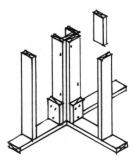

Use straight studs for door openings; it will make life easier for the "finish" man. Run the cripples to the deck so that the bottom plate butts up to it. Nail two nails into the bottom plate and two at the top, then stagger a nail at each side of the cripple in between. This will keep the 2 × 4 from twisting, and it leaves a more stable base to shim the door jambs from. Double nailing and alternating sides when face nailing is a good way to keep things solid. If nailed in the middle only, the piece tends to cup and rock.

After all the partitions are in and the door openings cut, nail 2 × 4 blocks (6-to-8-inch scrap) in all the corners and each side of the door openings. This will give good backing for the baseboards.

It has been said that "a good framer is worth two finish men." If a house is well framed, the finish work goes so easy; if poorly framed, you struggle and fudge over and over.

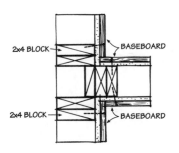

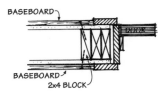

CHAPTER THIRTEEN

Roof Framing

Rafter lengths and angles are most accurately obtained by drawing them on the deck. If the second floor has no deck, then the place to lay them out is on the first floor—before the walls go up. There are many "rafter rules" and rafter tables that do a fine job. The framing square is another good tool for the job; but if you have a deck to work off, it is foolproof. Make sure that both ends of the deck are equal in length. If rafters are to go alongside joists, this measurement has already been done with the walls below. If there is to be a plate on top of the deck at the edges, snap a chalk line for the plate to nail to.

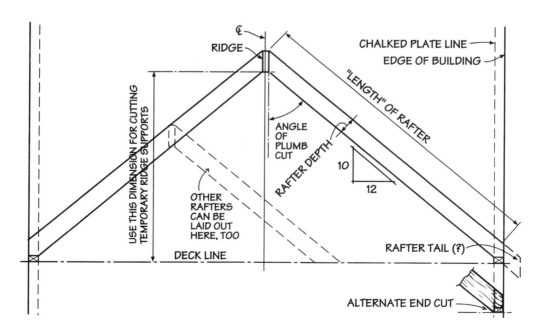

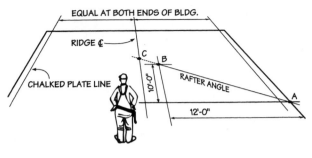

EQUAL AT BOTH ENDS OF BLDG.

RIDGE ℄

CHALKED PLATE LINE

C B

10'-0"

RAFTER ANGLE

A

12'-0"

Snap the center line and a base line perpendicular to it. From the roof pitch (10 in 12 for example), establish the angle. Snap a chalk line from point "A" through point "B," crossing center line at point "C." This is the rafter angle. Complete the layout.

Transfer angle, with bevel square or protractor, to a piece of straight rafter stock.

Mark an "X" on the top to avoid confusion (*even if it is straight*). Cut the top "plumb cut" only on a pair of straight pieces of rafter stock. Check how they fit over the deck layout. When the fit is good, lay out the rest of the rafter on one piece only. Cut and check with layout on deck. When match is good, cut and mark both pieces with the word PATTERN. Save these "patterns" and two other straight pieces for the end rafters. It will help when trimming with rake boards.

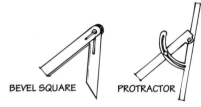

BEVEL SQUARE   PROTRACTOR

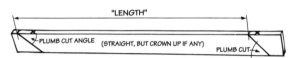

"LENGTH"

PLUMB CUT ANGLE   (STRAIGHT, BUT CROWN UP IF ANY)   PLUMB CUT

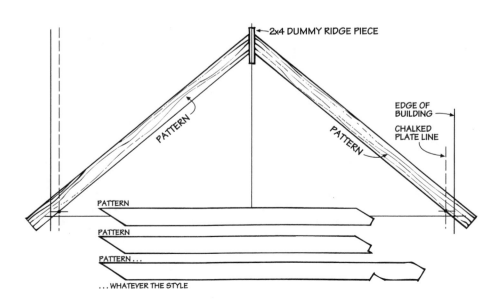

2x4 DUMMY RIDGE PIECE

PATTERN   PATTERN

EDGE OF BUILDING

CHALKED PLATE LINE

PATTERN

PATTERN

PATTERN...

...WHATEVER THE STYLE

The radial arm saw is the quickest way to cut rafters. Use the "pattern" as a guide for setting the angle and length.

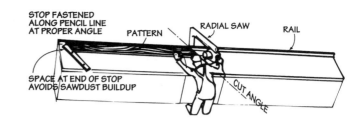

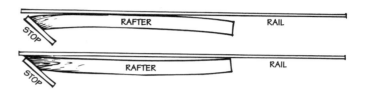

When setting stops, leave a space between rail and stop. This keeps sawdust from building up against the edge, which would change the length of the cut piece.

Cut rafters with crown away from the rail. Avoid using bad pieces; they cause all sorts of problems.

Using an angle T square and tape measure is another way to cut rafters. Best to use a "measuring stick," the length of the rafter, for measuring (hard to read the wrong length on this stick). The T square is made of ¼-inch plywood and a 2 × 4. Hold it against the rafter (or tack hold), then cut with power saw against the angled edge.

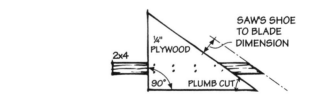

Still another way is to use the pattern to trace on each piece and cut freehand with power saw or handsaw. The bird's mouth and other cuts are done with a power saw after marking with a jig made up of rafter stock and plywood. Any combination of these can be used.

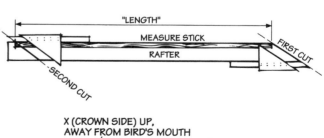

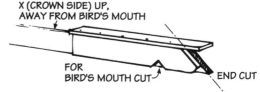

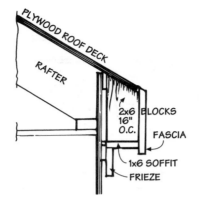

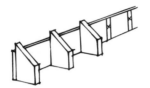

If a short overhang is used, blocks cut from the rafter ends can be used (they are the right angle, too). This method creates a nice straight line for the fascia and soffit, and it doesn't matter if there are any irregularities in the rafter ends. It can sometimes mean using the next-shorter-size rafter stock (a 14 footer instead of a 16-footer). Run the blocks through a table saw to even them up in length and width. The blocks are nailed on a 1 × 6 or 1 × 8 at rafter locations. Three or four of these sections are made up on the ground.

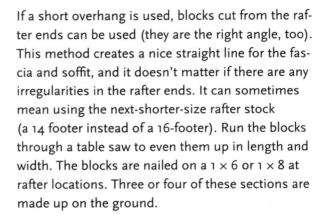

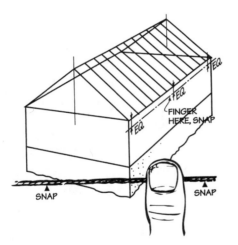

Locate the bottom of the blocks at each end and at the middle of the building. Stretch a chalk line the length of the building and snap it. If the line is long, hold the string against the wall with your finger, and snap each side of your fingered string. Always finger a long line, particularly on a windy day or if it is on a sidewall. Otherwise, the string will not snap true; also, a long line will not show at the other end of the snap.

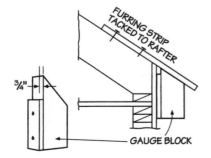

Use a gauge block at each end and in the middle for locating a chalk line.

A piece of 1 × 6 or 1 × 8 fence board with a U-brace at the upper end will support the ridge at one end. Another brace on the deck, fastened to the rafter scaffolding, supports the other. As the rafters go up, the scaffolding is moved along. Scaffolding can also be built the full length of the deck.

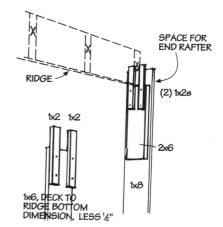

It is easier to put cleats on top of the planks—no problem with tripping.

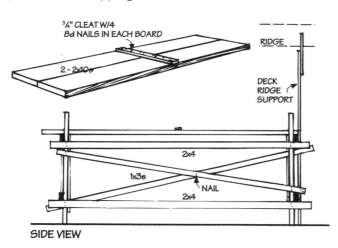

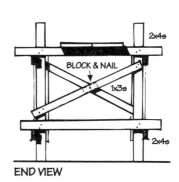

Cut ridge pieces to fit the length of the building. Lay them on the deck to make sure they are of the correct total length, outside face of stud to outside face of stud. Mark the rafter locations by laying the ridge along the ceiling joists (or the edge plate, if used).

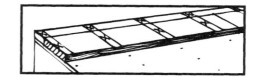

Nail the first end ridge support centered on the face of the end wall. The seat should be ½ inch less than the height of the ridge bottom (dimension on rafter layout on deck). A hand level for plumbing this support will do. The rafter scaffolding, with the short ridge support nailed at one end, should be in place.

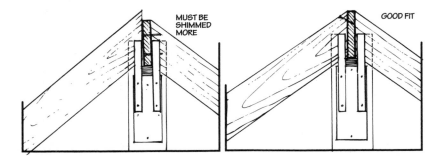

MUST BE SHIMMED MORE

GOOD FIT

With the first ridge piece laid up on the supports, shimmed to the approximate height, one rafter is nailed in place. Shim the ridge to its correct height with the opposite rafter in place. Make sure the straight end pieces you saved are used here.

After the section of rafters is in, it is a good time to plumb the ridge end; but pick a calm day. A moderate wind is okay if there are calm spells. The plumb bob is the best instrument for this job. Loop the string over a nail in the ridge end, then control the bob height with one hand so it just clears the deck and steady it with the other. With the staging moved to the next section, it will be easy to adjust the first section to the plumb position. Secure with a diagonal brace from ridge to deck.

The next ridge piece is butted, toenailed, and cleated to the first-section ridge piece. After all rafters are in, they are straightened just like the joists: shimmed string on end-rafter faces, straighten, and diagonal brace. The in-between rafters are eyeballed straight and held with furring strips. A chalk line, fingered in the middle and at 48 inches up from the rafter ends, is snapped for the first row of plywood to be nailed to. Since no water can collect here, the plywood sheets are laid up tight.

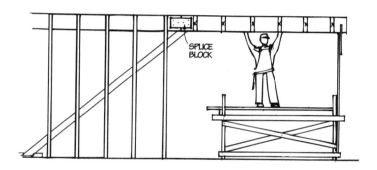

Tack the first row to make sure all is going right. If the first row is done right, the rest of the sheets will go well.

Exterior Trim

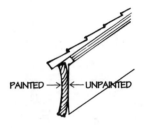

PAINTED →|←— UNPAINTED

Back-prime all exterior trim before cutting it to length to keep it from picking up moisture and cupping severely. The paint will suck into the wood nicely if thinned quite a bit. Paint exposed ends and butted ends to keep moisture out; the trim will last longer. Do not use clear preservative as a primer unless you can wait a few weeks for drying. Paint over preservative takes a long time to dry. If raw wood must go up, put preservative on to keep the surface from drying and cracking. Preservative irritates the eyes, so keep your hands away from your face even long after painting.

If unpainted trim sits even a few hours in the sun, it will dry and cup, ultimately splitting.

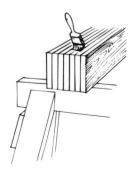

Stack boards together on edge to paint edges first. Then lay them down for painting the faces.

Space with either thin strips of wood ¼ inch square or 10d nails. Use as many as necessary to keep boards apart.

The garage is a good place to set up painting racks; it's spacious and under cover.

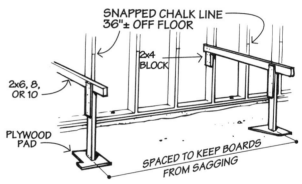

SNAPPED CHALK LINE 36"± OFF FLOOR

2x4 BLOCK

2x6, 8, OR 10

PLYWOOD PAD

SPACED TO KEEP BOARDS FROM SAGGING

Oil-base paint needs good air circulation. ½-inch-square strips for stickers work best.

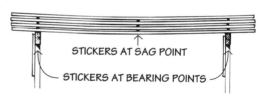

STICKERS AT SAG POINT

STICKERS AT BEARING POINTS

Painting the edges of a stack of clapboards with a brush speeds up this job.

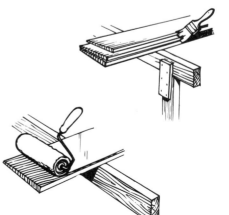

Painting the faces with a roller (back first then turn board over to roll the face) really speeds things up.

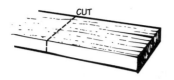

When trimming the exterior of a building, check the ends of the boards for cracks. They will sometimes be very thin lines. If there is a crack, cut off an inch past where the crack begins.

Check the end for poor milling and cut it off.

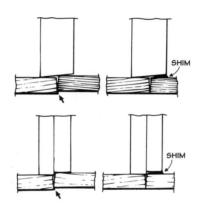

When butting two pieces of trim, the surfaces sometimes are not flush. Shim the low piece with pieces of 15-lb. felt building paper or wood-shingle tips.

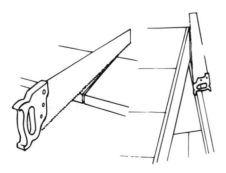

To make good fitting joints on exterior trim, run a handsaw through the joint after the initial cut is made and pieces are tacked in place. It might take two or three cuts. For wood gutters use a very coarse saw. You can't always get a saw into the joints, and in such cases they will have to be trimmed with a sharp block plane.

Check boards for cupping and put the cup face in; the joints stay tighter that way. Wood shrinks on the sapwood or barkside, causing cupping on that surface. In cabinet work the sapwood is kept on the inside surface of the work.

Straight butted ends are cut with the visible face and bottom tight and the back and top open or relieved.

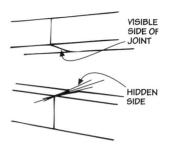

VISIBLE SIDE OF JOINT

HIDDEN SIDE

The same principle applies to corner boards wherever one edge butts up to the other face. Use a slight bevel on a table saw or hand plane. Be sure to mark the bevel edge; it's sometimes difficult to tell at a glance.

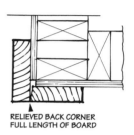

RELIEVED BACK CORNER FULL LENGTH OF BOARD

When planing a bevel on long boards, use a 24-inch jointing plane.

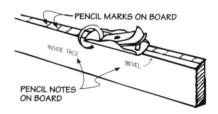

PENCIL MARKS ON BOARD

INSIDE FACE

BEVEL

PENCIL NOTES ON BOARD

When butting boards on a 1½-inch member, use thin wire nails (6d common or 8d box nail), and angle them away from the joint.

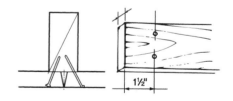

1½"

If you must nail close to the edge, dull the nail point with a few hammer blows. A pointed nail pushes the fibers apart, causing a split; but a blunt-end nail tears a hole as it goes through.

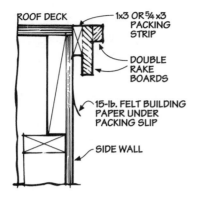

ROOF DECK

1x3 OR 5/4 x3 PACKING STRIP

DOUBLE RAKE BOARDS

15-lb. FELT BUILDING PAPER UNDER PACKING SLIP

SIDE WALL

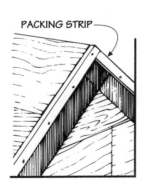

PACKING STRIP

RAKE BOARD

SHINGLES OR CLAPBOARDS

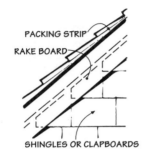

PACKING STRIP

COMPONENTS OF EXTERIOR TRIM

1. Packing strip for rake members; keep strip short to allow for ear board
2. Fascia
3. Gutter and gutter return with water table
4. Rake boards
5. Soffit
6. Frieze board packing
7. Frieze board
8. Corner boards
9. Miscellaneous trim
10. Ridge boards

1. The rake board is packed out so that clapboards and shingles can tuck up behind. A 1 × 3 furring strip is used if 3/4-inch corner boards are used. It is a little tight with shingles that measure 7/8 of an inch from sheathing to face of butts, but it will work (split shakes are much thicker). Use 5/4 inch × 3 for 5/4-inch corner boards. Yes 3/4 inch will work; but the ear board will have to be trimmed to 3/4 inch, behind the rake only, to receive it.

2. The fascia is bevel cut on top to match the roof pitch and mitered at one end for ear board return. If rake board covers the corner of ear board and fascia, mitering is not necessary.

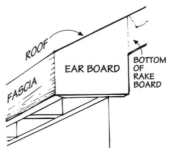

ROOF

FASCIA

EAR BOARD

BOTTOM OF RAKE BOARD

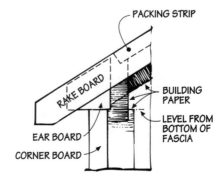

PACKING STRIP

RAKE BOARD

BUILDING PAPER

LEVEL FROM BOTTOM OF FASCIA

EAR BOARD

CORNER BOARD

Ear board should be level on the bottom and should have a notch cut in the back to receive the top tongue of the corner board. Paint all cuts.

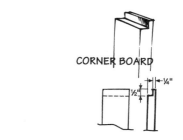

BACK

FACE

(CORNER BOARD)

¾" CORNER BOARD

¾"

½

⁵/₁₆"

Corner board tucks under ear board.

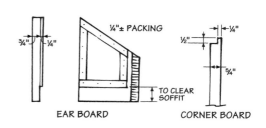

CORNER BOARD

¼"

½"

⁵/₄-inch corner board needs ³/₄-inch ear board with ¼-inch packing strips.

A strip of 15-lb. felt is stapled behind rake and ear board. Use a piece wide enough so that paper on sidewalls can be easily slid under.

¾" ¼"

¼"± PACKING

TO CLEAR SOFFIT

EAR BOARD

¼"

½"

⁵/₄"

CORNER BOARD

Mitering exterior trim with a handsaw is not difficult. The outside corner and the bottom miter line are all that is visible. Start with a good miter cut on the bottom and follow the outside line across the board. At the same time push the saw off the inside line, which will open the inside of the miter cut, making for a good, tight fit outside. If the angle is off, all that has to be adjusted is the small section of the bottom miter.

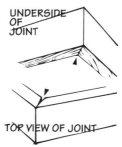

UNDERSIDE OF JOINT

TOP VIEW OF JOINT

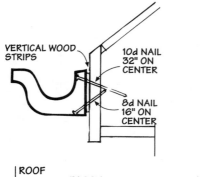

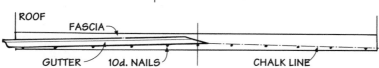

3. The gutter either returns on the ear board or butts against the rake. In both cases it should be separated from the fascia with wood strips to prevent rotting. Slope the gutter from middle to ends on long runs. Snap a chalk line and then tack 10d nails on the line to support the gutter while fitting. Sometimes the gable trim limits the slope; just be sure water will not puddle.

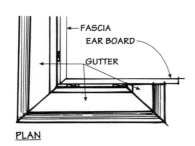

Miter the gutter and the gutter returns in a miter box or freehand. Miter only one end of the return and make sure it is plenty long. Tack in place, level, and inspect the fit. Run a coarse sharp saw through the cut as many times as is necessary for a good fit. Now miter the other end and its little return. The top of the gutter returns will have to be trimmed for the water table to lay flat.

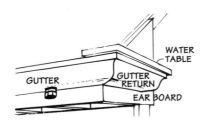

Lead the ends and drill downspout holes with a hole drill in an electric drill or a brace and bit. A nylon plumbing nipple screwed into a hole a tad smaller will not rust out like a galvanized nipple will.

Lead laid in gutter up onto roof and water table keeps water out of the gutter return.

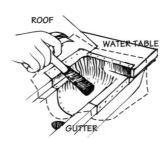

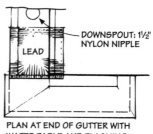

PLAN AT END OF GUTTER WITH WATER TABLE AND FLASHING ADDED

Keep creases out by working lead with hammer handle. Hammer on wood block to tuck lead into corners, being careful not to puncture lead. Use a large piece of lead and trim to fit after shaping. Caulk and nail.

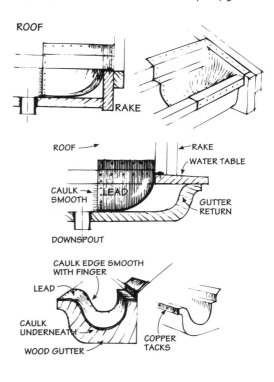

If gutter ends at rake board (no gutter return), treat the same way in gutter and run the lead up to, and lapped on top of, the rake board.

Lead middle mitered joint 3 inches each side of joint.

4. Choose straight boards for the rake if possible. If necessary, however, some bending can be pulled out. With double rake members, the lapped peak is best for tying the whole business together.

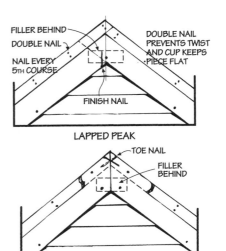

Plumb cuts must be cut carefully and nailed securely.

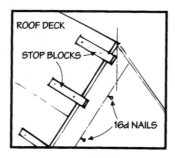

Nail stop blocks on roof and two 16d nails into the side of the building at the bottom line of the rake board. One person can work the rake by resting the board on the nails. Tack in place while getting dimensions and fit.

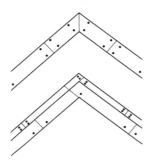

Use a sharp block plane to make the fine fits. If a rake is too long to do in one piece, put the short pieces at the peak end; it's not as visible from the ground. With double members, stagger the joints. Run a handsaw through joints, where possible, to get good joints. Pull rake up to be flush with roof top—strong if anything, not weak. Asphalt shingles look bad sagging down, and wood shingles will split if pulled down too far.

5. The soffit is put on like the fascia. Both ends of each piece are eased back (beveled on the back face).

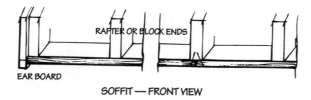

SOFFIT — FRONT VIEW

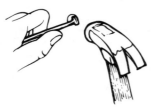

Set all nails used in exterior trim; it pulls the pieces up tight. Putty nail holes before painting. Use your largest nail set for common nails; if stuck without one, use a nail on its side.

Double nail on the bottom. Nail through the fascia as needed.

Wherever the soffit needs pulling in, a pry bar behind is sometimes needed to persuade the piece over. Pull over, nail bottom, then nail front.

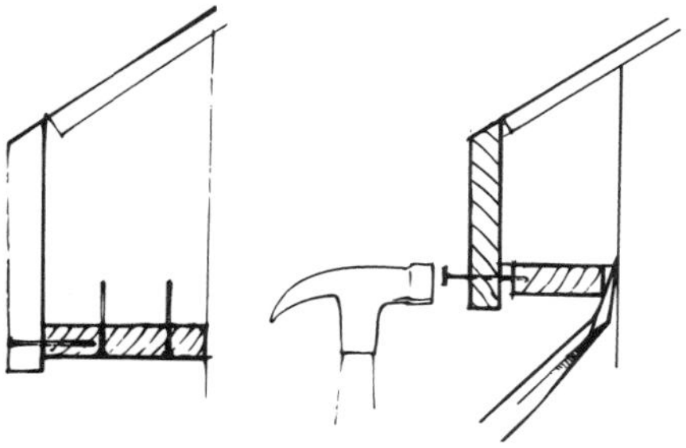

One person can install long sections of trim by using a simple wood L-shaped helper.

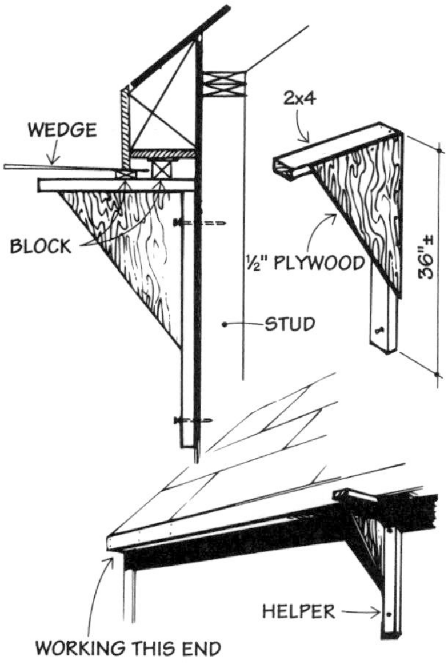

WEDGE

BLOCK

2x4

½" PLYWOOD

36" ±

STUD

HELPER

WORKING THIS END

Nailing the fascia board to soffit when a continuous soffit vent is used works best when it is backed with a removable block spacer and forced over with a flat bar.

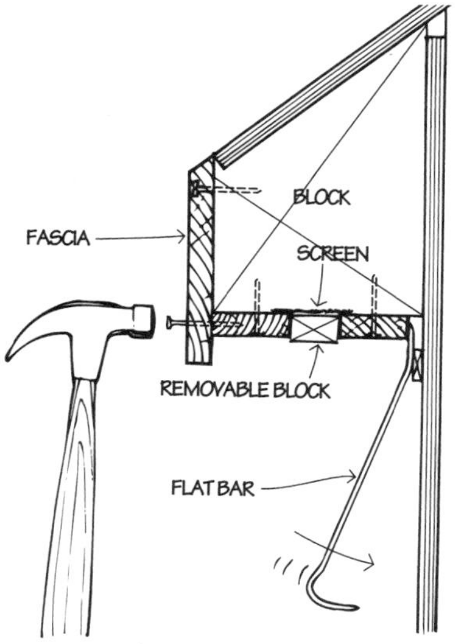

FASCIA

BLOCK

SCREEN

REMOVABLE BLOCK

FLAT BAR

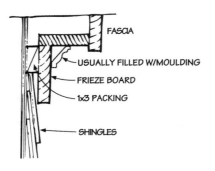

FASCIA

USUALLY FILLED W/MOULDING

FRIEZE BOARD

1x3 PACKING

SHINGLES

6. and 7. The frieze board is packed out with a 1 × 3 just like the rakes so that the siding tops will fit behind. It's neater and easier, and the shingles won't split and fall out.

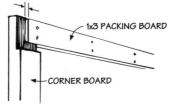

1x3 PACKING BOARD

CORNER BOARD

Keep the ends in from the corners to allow for the corner board.

15-LB. FELT SPLINE STRIPS

8. Fifteen-pound felt spline strips are stapled in place before trim boards are put on. For corners, a piece of building paper (15-lb. felt) is wrapped around the corner extending 4 inches past each corner board on the sides and bottom. Fold the paper down the middle before stapling up. All paper spline strips should be cut at the same time. If you need 144 feet of 12-inch splines (the length of a 15-lb. felt roll), cut it off the end of a roll with a power saw. A 9-inch saw won't quite reach through one-half of the roll. Make sure all lapping paper has the upper piece over the lower piece for water runoff.

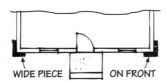

WIDE PIECE   ON FRONT

The narrow corner board piece goes on the side of the building. The wider corner board goes on the face of the building as you look at the front door from the outside.

The narrow corner board piece is nailed on first, keeping it snug against the stops (similar to putting on a rake board). 8d common nails are used for trim nailing with an occasional finish nail and brad.

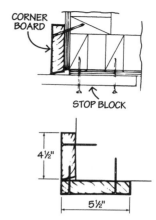

The wider piece is next. Keep it flush against, and even with, the edge of the narrow one.

Nail at the top first, working down. The wide piece is also nailed at the top, working down at the corner edge only. Make sure the pieces are flush. Then nail the edge that is away from the corner. Set all nails to pull pieces together. Sometimes a 10d common is needed to pull the corners together.

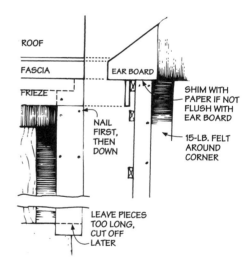

The wide board usually swells, so a touch up with a sharp block plane will be needed.

The corner boards are left long until after the siding is put on. They are then squared across with a combination square and cut with a handsaw.

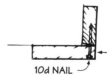

9. Miscellaneous trim goes in as needed.

10. The ridge boards are handled just like corner boards except for the angle.

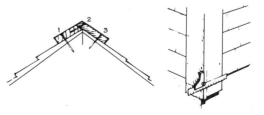

FRIEZE

EAR BOARD

Preassembling corner boards is a good idea whenever installing them.

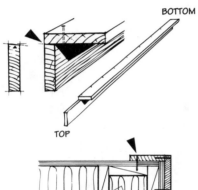

BOTTOM

TOP

The narrow board should be beveled to create a tight joint at the outside face.

Adjust the tops to reach the ear board and frieze board.

This outside corner has plenty of solid wood for nailing corner boards in place. There is also access for insulating at the corner.

This corner cannot be insulated easily, and the nailing for one of the corner boards is not good.

Roofing

When building a house, get the roof on as soon as possible, unless you want the summer sun to dry green framing lumber. With the roof on, the building becomes a good place to work and store material out of the weather. With windows and doors installed, the house can also be locked up.

This is a comfortable setup for roofing with either wood or asphalt shingles. The wall-bracket scaffolding is there to start the roof from and provides a good place to keep supplies for the roof work. Later it can be used for loading up the roof scaffolding with shingles.

Red cedar is the best material for a wood-shingle roof. Some people suffer severe infections from red-cedar splinters—nothing to worry about, but be aware.

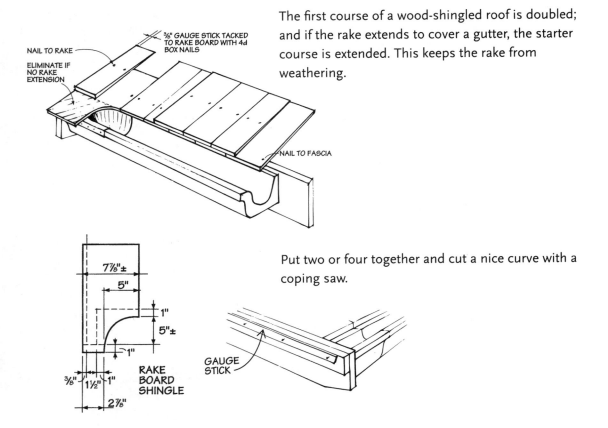

NAIL TO RAKE

ELIMINATE IF
NO RAKE
EXTENSION

⅜" GAUGE STICK TACKED
TO RAKE BOARD WITH 4d
BOX NAILS

NAIL TO FASCIA

The first course of a wood-shingled roof is doubled; and if the rake extends to cover a gutter, the starter course is extended. This keeps the rake from weathering.

7⅞"±

5"

1"

5"±

1"

⅜" 1½" 1"

2⅞"

RAKE
BOARD
SHINGLE

Put two or four together and cut a nice curve with a coping saw.

GAUGE
STICK

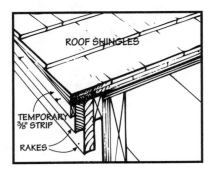

ROOF SHINGLES

TEMPORARY
⅜" STRIP

RAKES

Make sure the $3/8$-inch-gauge sticks are tacked on the rakes to allow for overhang.

$3/8$-inch overhang at the rake
1-inch overhang at the eaves

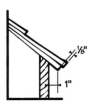

⅜"

1"

Nail the rake-board shingles at each end and one shingle in the middle of the roof. All will be positioned with a 1-inch overhang at the eaves. Stretch a string from end to end and tack below the bottom edge of the shingles. The middle shingle is to support the string in a long span. Keeping the string below the shingle bottom lets the shingles be placed close to, but not touching, the string. If a shingle touches the string, the line moves down; if another touches, the line moves down some more. Eyeball along the bottom to be sure all is well.

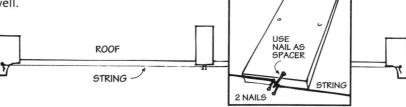

Wood shingles are usually laid with 5- to 5¼-inch courses. A roofing stick with shingle gauges is made up with that in mind. The sticks are made of straight 1 × 3 × 12-, 14-, or 16-foot furring strips, as many as it takes to reach the length of the roof.

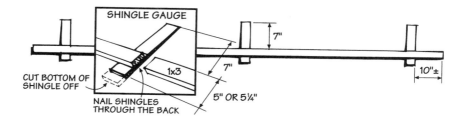

Start with the second course, using the roofing sticks by lining up the bottoms of the shingle gauges with the course below. This will give an automatic 5-inch or 5¼-inch course. Nail the very tip of the gauge to the roof with a wood-shingle nail.

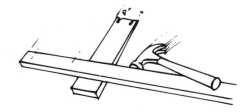

The stick is removed by tapping it with a hammer, which leaves the nail in the roof.

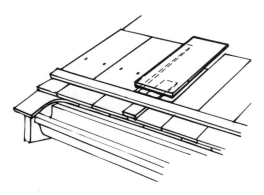

With the sticks secured along the full length of the roof, just lay the shingles with the butts against the 1 x 3 and nail. Lay as many as is comfortable and then nail, but do not nail the shingle that is over the gauge unless it spans by quite a bit. It will either split or the gauge shingle will get nailed. Make sure the shingles don't slide under the stick. It is very easy to skip a course, so keep checking.

Even though the shingles are wet, space them loosely; don't squeeze them in. Some moisture will be picked up, and they will swell and buckle. If an old batch of very dry shingles is used, ⅛-inch spacing is recommended. Wide shingles should be used; but after nailing them into place, cut the surface where you want them to split. Nail each side of the cut.

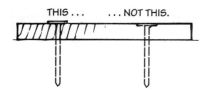

THIS ...   ... NOT THIS.

Red-cedar shingles are long lasting and a little harder than white cedar. Do not drive the nails hard, just enough to snug the shingle to the roof. On the last stroke, hold back a little. The nail should not be driven below the surface of the shingle or the shingle will crack. Be aware of cracked shingles as you use them. If you are uncertain, bend the shingle; the crack will show. Discard if bad.

There is an up and a down on a shingle; eyeball down the edge and see. The curve is very slight, but it is important to put the hump up. If not, shingles ski up.

Shingle joints should be a minimum 1½ inches offset on each course and 1 inch every third course to prevent leaks.

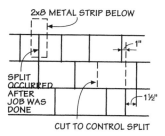

Roof brackets with 2 × 10 planks for staging are the most comfortable to work from. Locate brackets over rafters for secure nailing. As the staging is advanced up the roof, be aware of the courses into which the brackets must go. Fit the shingle, but leave it out. Tuck the tip under a shingle nearby.

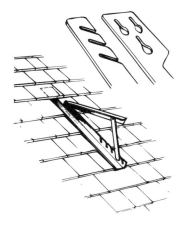

Fifteen-pound felt on the roof under the shingles will further prevent roof leaks. On new work, lay only as much paper as is required for the day's work. An evening moisture will wrinkle the paper severely, making it tough to shingle over.

Check dimensions from eaves to last course, at both ends and middle. Adjust course as necessary, reducing the course if 16-inch shingles are used. If using 18-inch shingles, then an increase will be all right. It is a good idea to snap a chalk line every once in a while to straighten things out. Keep a check, as you get near the ridge, for parallel and shingle-course dimensions. Figure where the bottom of the ridge board will go, then measure to the last shingle course laid to decide on any adjusting needed. A 2-inch final course looks bad.

When the shingling is finished, check the roof for splits that line up and mark with a pencil. Cut some 2 × 8 metal strips to slip under each split.

Asphalt shingles without cutouts are the faster to install and should last longer. The first place to wear on 3-tab shingles is in the cutout.

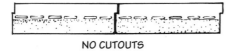

NO CUTOUTS

CUTOUTS OR 3-TAB SHINGLE

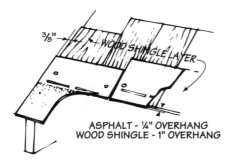

3/8" WOOD SHINGLE LAYER

ASPHALT - ¼" OVERHANG
WOOD SHINGLE - 1" OVERHANG

Wood-shingle starters at the eaves make a nicer looking job than metal strips. The roof is started just like the wood-shingle roof, with a 1-inch wood-shingle overhang. Building paper with lines is a big help in keeping the courses straight; so put the paper on with care, keeping edges running parallel with the eaves.

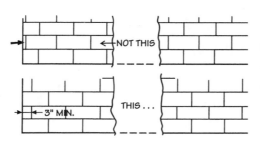

NOT THIS

THIS ...

3" MIN.

Measure the length of the roof so that the shingle layout will eliminate a thin shingle strip at the gable ends. With tab shingles, the tabs at each end look best when equal.

All asphalt shingles have marks for alignment. Follow the marks but keep an eye on the paper underneath and adjust to it, provided the paper has been put on parallel to the eaves.

All the starter-course shingles are cut and installed according to the instructions on the bundles. Tack the first asphalt-shingle course in place, with a ¼-inch eave overhang on the wood shingles, according to the layout arrived at earlier. Frequently these layouts turn out wrong and are easier to change if the nails are not driven home. A piece of asphalt shingle has to be cut to cover the rake-board shingle. Make sure the ³/₈-inch-gauge strip is tacked on the rake. Too much asphalt-shingle overhang tends to sag.

After the shingle layout is established, vertical lines are snapped from ridge to eaves. These offset lines are only used with tab shingles. These lines keep the cutouts aligned up the roof. Shingles without cutouts should be staggered randomly. There is also a random stagger for cutout shingles that looks good.

Roof brackets and 2 x 10 planks are the most comfortable to work from and good for stacking bundles on. As the ridge is approached, provide for full 5-inch courses all the way. If the paper was laid parallel to the eaves, use it as a guide for straightness, along with an occasional eyeball down the course. A few chalk lines for the last few courses are a must to bring them in line with the ridge. Don't be too fussy on the roof; you can't see the imperfections from the ground. Only at the ridge is it noticeable. Be very concerned with the prevention of leaks.

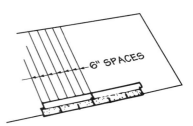

The gable ends can be either cut off as the course is worked on or cut when finished along a snapped chalk line. The 3/8-inch-gauge strip is used as a guide for cutting as you go. Starter pieces can be cut and worked from one end. If they are cut as you go, lay the shingle in place, reach under and mark with nail, turn over, and cut with knife or tin snips.

Divide a full shingle into thirds to get the cap pattern. Cut the ends away from the butt, tapered, so that, when they fold over the ridge, the corners won't stick out. Take one of the caps and mark PATTERN on it. Lay it on the back side of a full shingle and cut with a utility knife. Use the pattern as a guide for the knife. Keep caps warm for easy folding.

Snap a line for one side of the ridge and nail caps to it. Keep caps warm and install them on a sunny day; the caps will crack if folded over on a cold day. Nail one side of each cap and, if it is warm, bend it over and nail the other side. If not, nail them all on one side and let the sun work for you. Bend and nail when they are warm.

If shingles must be carried up a ladder, carry them on your shoulder.

Tip bundle to groin area. Left hand is to the body side of the center line of the bundle. The right hand is away from the center line.

Drive hips forward and, at the same time, pull with arms to final resting place, the right shoulder.

Siding

Any wood can be used for shingles, but in New England white cedar is the first choice because of its beautiful graying quality. Red cedar ages a not-so-pretty brown. Hand-split shakes are usually red cedar and much thicker. Some of what follows applies to clapboards too. White cedars are flat sawn about $3/8$ inch at the butt and 16 inches long. When buying shingles, buy a brand name. They might cost a little more, but they will be worth it in time saved. Try a trial bundle or two to see how they go up. They should sit one next to the other, with an occasional trimming required. They might go better right to left or left to right. When you find a good brand, stick with them. They are graded clears and extras, the extras being the better of the two.

Mark the various horizontal interruptions the walls have on a story pole. Start with the front of the building.

Mark the corner boards and door casings. Go light with the pencil.

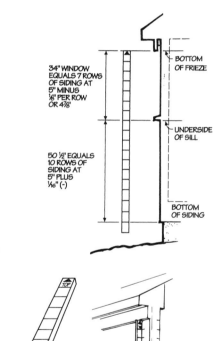

34" WINDOW EQUALS 7 ROWS OF SIDING AT 5" MINUS 1/8" PER ROW OR 4 7/8"

BOTTOM OF FRIEZE

UNDERSIDE OF SILL

50 1/2" EQUALS 10 ROWS OF SIDING AT 5" PLUS 1/16" (-)

BOTTOM OF SIDING

TOP

WDW

BOT.

The shingles might need some adjusting around the corner, but usually windows are set at the same height. There might be a short kitchen or bath window. See if the same spacing works.

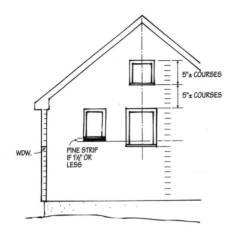

5"± COURSES

5"± COURSES

PINE STRIP
IF 1½" OR
LESS

WDW.

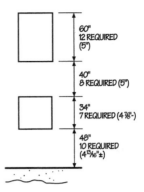

60"
12 REQUIRED
(5")

40"
8 REQUIRED (5")

34"
7 REQUIRED (4⅞"-)

48"
10 REQUIRED
(4¹³⁄₁₆"±)

White cedars are 16 inches, so stretching much past 5 inches loses triple coverage—better to reduce. 5⅛ inches or 5³⁄₁₆ inches will do if indeed the shingles are 16 inches, but many bundles have quite a few "shorts."

Start with building paper stapled to the wall and tucked under the door and corner splines. Keep the bottom of the paper at the bottom edge of the shingles.

PAPER SPLINE

15-LB. FELT (PAPER)

DOUBLE COURSE
ON BOTTOM

SINGLE
COUSES

The shingles can be laid to the bottom of the paper edge or on a 1 × 3 stick with metal strips hung on the wall.

15-LB. FELT (PAPER)

1x3

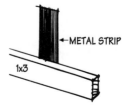

METAL STRIP

1x3

Snap a chalk line from corner to corner for the start of the next course. Tack one or two 1 × 3 furring strips to that chalk line. Use 4d box nails high on the 1 × 3. The small wire nail won't leave a big hole in the shingle, and, if it is high on the course, it will be less noticeable.

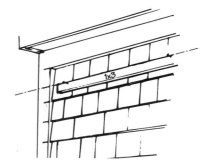

When face-nailing shingles that tuck up under the frieze, windows, or rakes, use galvanized 5d box nails. They look better and hold better if nails are in a straight line and set with a nail set. The shadow line of the frieze, window sill, or rake can be used as a guideline. Otherwise, a light pencil line, with a gauge stick as a guide, will do.

FRIEZE   WINDOW SILL   RAKE

On short runs use a level to mark the line for a short 1 × 3.

For inside corners use $^3/_4$ × 1 to keep shingle butts from clashing. A 1 × 1 will do, but it will be more noticeable.

SHINGLES DO NOT QUITE TOUCH

¾" × 1"
TOTAL SHINGLE THICKNESS: 1"

INSIDE CORNER

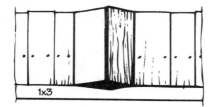

White cedars can be laid up tight; there are no dry ones, so they will shrink. In fact the two last shingles in a course can be angled, like shuffling cards, and snapped in.

Trial and error will show how strong the snap can be to make this work.

snapped 'er too hard again, didn't he?

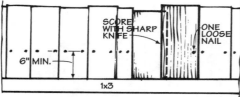

Work both ends to the middle. Two workers, a lefty and a righty, make a good combination. Lap the last pair of shingles, score with a knife, break, and put back in; they should fit. Usually there is a shingle that fits perfectly after a little shave with a sharp knife or hatchet. Singles should fit against casings, and a block plane helps them fit.

"IN" FACES

White cedars have "in" and "out" faces. Look for the curve and put the hump out. It's very slight, but it's there.

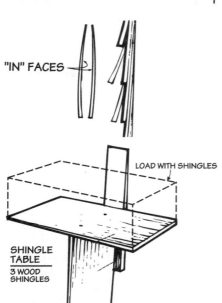

LOAD WITH SHINGLES

SHINGLE TABLE
3 WOOD SHINGLES

A shingle table is used to avoid the need for reaching for shingles when in a difficult position or on a ladder. Two or three tables around the job are all that are needed. Slip the tip under a shingle course and load with shingles.

The first course of wood sidewall shingles can be laid on a 1 × 3 stick that has a few support, or hanger, shingles nailed to it.

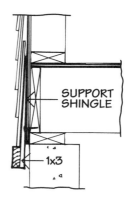

SUPPORT SHINGLE

1x3

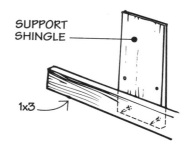

SUPPORT SHINGLE

1x3

The support, or hanger, shingles are permanently nailed in place as one of the underneath starter-course shingles. When the shingling is finished, the 1 × 3 is removed and the protruding shingle butts are cut off with a handsaw or utility knife.

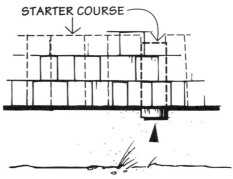

STARTER COURSE

Many shingles can be set in place before nailing them when a Mason's line is stretched along the tips. Mason's line blocks work well at trim and corners. Finish nails in the trim work as well.

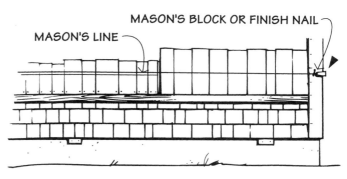

MASON'S BLOCK OR FINISH NAIL

MASON'S LINE

Joint spacing is not critical on sidewalls, but they still should not line up. A 1½-inch minimum at each course should be held. The third course is not too critical.

SILL

MIN. ½" TO MAX. ⅝"

Window sills are usually not rabbeted enough to receive the shingles. Use a ½-inch minimum; a ⅝-inch rabbet is better. Widen the rabbet on all the windows at the same time before installing them.

Use narrow shingles against corners and casings. Wide shingles shrink too much, leaving gaps at these points. Be aware of bad shingles, splits, and bad spots or very hard ones. Discard the hard shingles; they will curl badly and split. Splits in white cedars are generally throwaways.

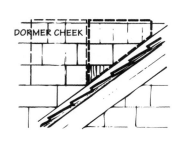

DORMER CHEEK

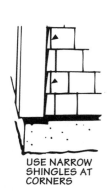

USE NARROW SHINGLES AT CORNERS

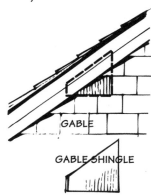

GABLE

GABLE SHINGLE

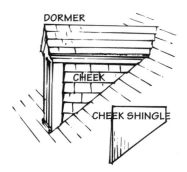

DORMER

CHEEK

CHEEK SHINGLE

Save wide shingles ("bedsheets") for gables and dormer cheeks.

Cut all cheek and gable shingles at the same time; it's easy enough to figure how many. A table or radial saw is best for this job, but a handsaw or power saw will cut through a stack of them.

To put in or replace a shingle in a completed shingle wall use a wood wedge, nail set, and box nails. Drive the shingle up to ½ inch from aligning with butts. Use a block, held at the butt, to hammer against. Pry up the shingle above and hold with wedges. Drive two 4d nails at an angle, set nails, and drive shingle to proper alignment. The upper shingle won't bend easily. Shingling up the gable end using metal wall brackets will leave a condition like this at each bracket.

To cut a quantity of shingles to a specific length (for under windows and frieze boards), cut them, while still in the bundle, with a power saw. Drop the bundle on its end to even the butts. Measure size on top of bundle, and count the layers combined with width of bundle for quantity. Eight layers at 20 inches equals 160 inches, or about 13 feet.

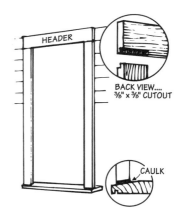

To keep casings water tight, the side casings should be rabbeted into the header. The sills should be caulked.

A clapboard jig is a must for getting good fits at corners, window trim, and door trim. The jig straddles the clapboard and is held hard against the trim while marking a cut line with a utility knife or sharp pencil.

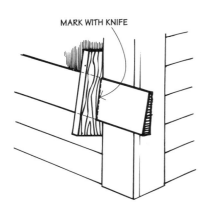

MARK WITH KNIFE

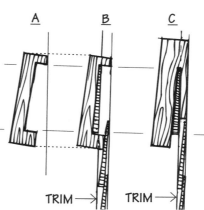

A B C

Ⓐ - THE JIG

Ⓑ - THE JIG STRADDLING THE CLAPBOARD AT CORNER OR TRIM

Ⓒ - ANOTHER JIG DESIGN

TRIM → TRIM →

At the End of the Day

TUESDAYS AND THURSDAYS...

... MONDAYS, WEDNESDAYS, AND FRIDAYS.

Secure the building at the end of the day. Take ladders down to prevent the winds from toppling them and to keep kids from climbing them. Batten down the paper that's on the building. That includes all the splines at corners, windows, and doors as well as roof and sidewalls. A strong wind will rip them off in a hurry. Wood-shingle tips, scraps, furring strips, or any scrap sticks tacked to the building will do the job. Tuck loose shingles, whether asphalt or wood, under unopened bundles. Rebind partly used wood-shingle bundles. Pick up paper wrappings and wood-shingle scraps; they love to fly with the wind to the neighbors' yards. There is a bonus to this clean up; many a lost tool is found.

Look over what was done and plan the next day's work. Try to complete each job stage—nailing off the deck, bridging, wall straightening—as you go. It is too easy to forget where you left off. It breaks continuity to have to come back to do this, and it is less efficient. Most of the time, postponed work does not get done. Check for incomplete job stages and plan to finish them the next day. Check the material on hand, and the material required for the next day's work. Double-check for tools left on the job. It is a good way to wind down, to save tools, and to get ready for a good start the next morning.

When winding up extension cords, alternate windings from day to day or week to week. Wind with the right hand one day and the left the next. It is particularly important with rubber cords because they will twist and split. The plastic cords simply get twisted and tangled, making unwinding difficult.

Some Safety Tips

Accidents, both personal and to the tools and building, are always preventable. Never leave a block of wood on the ground with a nail through it.

A good reason not to wear sneakers on the job

Fold it over or, better still, pull it. It won't dull a saw when you're cutting alongside a nail.

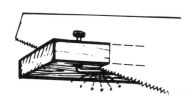

Nails are particularly hazardous at the end of long boards. They can rip open a hand or leg even when folded over. Any nails sticking out where there are people can do a job on clothes and skin. Doorways and hallways are not places for projecting nails.

Keep work areas in front of saws clear. Throw cut ends away into a scrap pile. Stumbling over blocks in front of a saw is not only dangerous, it is also aggravating; and when one is aggravated, one gets careless. Keep decks clear of 2 × 4 blocks; they are great ankle twisters.

Try to prevent wood braces from projecting too far out at about forehead height. It is a height that is easily missed with the eye but easily found with the head.

If a board must be there, hang a flag on it.

Clean up frequently; a clean job is a less accident-prone job.

Don't use tools beyond their capacity. A shovel is not a pry bar.

Miscellaneous Tips

This is a string-and-shim setup for straightening walls—
a simple loop to start at one end and the old-fashioned
"butcher's twist" at the other. That's what the old-time
butchers used to call it when they tied up their meat.

BUTCHER'S TWIST KNOT

¾" SHIM OR 10d NAIL

Pull string tight, then take up slack at nail. If you pull at
the nail, the line will break.

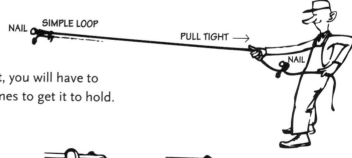

NAIL   SIMPLE LOOP   PULL TIGHT →

NAIL

If the string is to be pulled very tight, you will have to
repeat steps 3 and 4 two or three times to get it to hold.

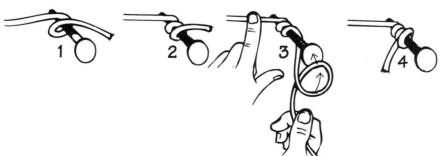

1   2   3   4

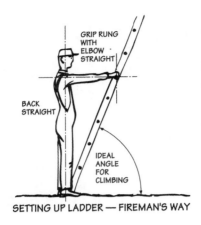

GRIP RUNG WITH ELBOW STRAIGHT

BACK STRAIGHT

IDEAL ANGLE FOR CLIMBING

SETTING UP LADDER — FIREMAN'S WAY

A ladder is an awkward thing to move, especially one with a long extension. It can be moved quite easily this way, even fully extended. It requires some balancing with arms, body, and head.

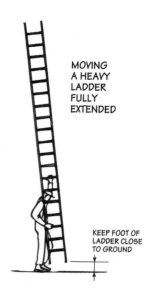

MOVING A HEAVY LADDER FULLY EXTENDED

KEEP FOOT OF LADDER CLOSE TO GROUND

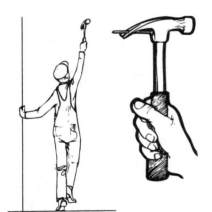

Every once in a while a nail must be located too high or too far from the work platform to be reached with both hands (one for holding the nail, one for the hammer). It can be sunk, though, if the nail is tucked in the claws of the hammer, with the nail head against the hammer neck and the nail pointing out. Some hammers accept a nail this way better than others; wedge the nail in, though, and it should stay. Then reach up and start the nail with a swing. Once it's held firmly by the wood, the hammer is reversed and the nail driven home.

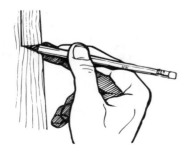

To draw a straight line, the thumb holds the pencil firmly against the pointer and middle fingers. For lines up to one inch from the edge, the middle finger rides along this edge.

For more accurate lines, use the combination square.

Scratch initials on tools for quick identification.

Lines up to four inches from the edge can be drawn using your little finger as the guide. Whatever finger you use, keep them all rigid by bracing them against each other.

CLINCHING A NAIL

To clinch a nail by simply folding it over will work, but a better way is to bend the tip and then fold it over, driving the tip into the wood. Be sure to back up the nail head with a piece of metal to keep the nail from being pushed back out while being folded over.

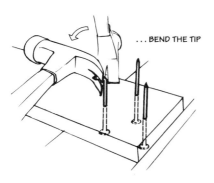

... BEND THE TIP

COMPLETE THE BEND ...

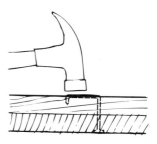

... FOLD OVER AND DRIVE HOME.

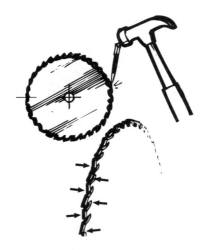

ROUGH SHARPEN & SETTING SAW BLADE

Even though a good carpenter has a good supply of sharp blades on the job, there is bound to be a time when a blade has to be sharpened on the job. To sharpen, support the blade, as close as possible to the tooth being dressed, and follow the existing angles with a firm forward stroke of the file. After sharpening, lay the blade on a piece of plywood and set every other tooth with a nail set and hammer. Turn the blade over and repeat on that side. The more set there is, the easier and rougher the cut.

There are many problems that crop up on a job that seem to have no solutions. Of course solutions are possible, but you never know where those solutions will come from, so be receptive to ideas. Also be aware of others' problems. You may have the solutions they need.

CROWN MOULDING

My dad told me of one situation with a problem that was solved in just that way. He was trimming out a dormer with crown moldings that met at the rake and eaves. The angle of the cut was impossible to figure. A fellow carpenter below looked up and said, "Eyeball and cut it." So my dad did it, and to his amazement it worked!

Then months later, on another job, the same fellow carpenter who had been below giving the advice was up against the same problem himself and was unable to solve it. This time my dad was below and said to him, "Eyeball and cut it." To the amazement of both parties, it worked again. You never know.

In concentrating on carpentry tricks of the trade, I have not shown or discussed many safety practices or devices, taking it for granted that basic procedures would be practiced by the reader. Safety goggles, protective clothing, safe ladders, temporary railings, and many other products and practices are part of good carpentry work. OSHA rules, manufacturers' instructions, building codes, and, most of all, common sense must take priority over hammers and nails in successful carpentry.

Cutting flashing is best done with a utility knife. A framing square, held against a partition plate that has been marked off for the flashing size, makes for square cuts of equal length.

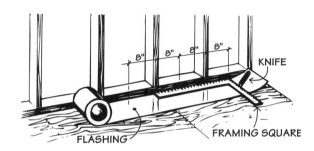

Any size nail can be started with this one-hand nailing method.

Hold a nail between the fingers with the nail head against the side of the hammer head. With one brisk swing, drive the point of the nail into the wood.

CHAPTER TWENTY

Saw Horses

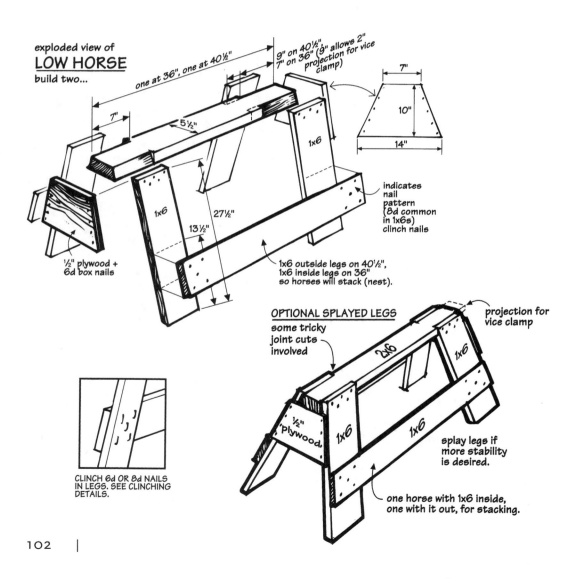

exploded view of
LOW HORSE
build two...

one at 36", one at 40½"

9" on 40½"
7" on 36" (9" allows 2"
projection for vice
clamp)

7"

5½"

1x6

7"

10"

14"

1x6

indicates
nail
pattern
(8d common
in 1x6s)
clinch nails

1x6

27½"

13½"

½" plywood +
6d box nails

1x6 outside legs on 40½",
1x6 inside legs on 36"
so horses will stack (nest).

OPTIONAL SPLAYED LEGS
some tricky
joint cuts
involved

projection for
vice clamp

2x6

1x6

½"
plywood

1x6

1x6

splay legs if
more stability
is desired.

CLINCH 6d OR 8d NAILS
IN LEGS. SEE CLINCHING
DETAILS.

one horse with 1x6 inside,
one with it out, for stacking.

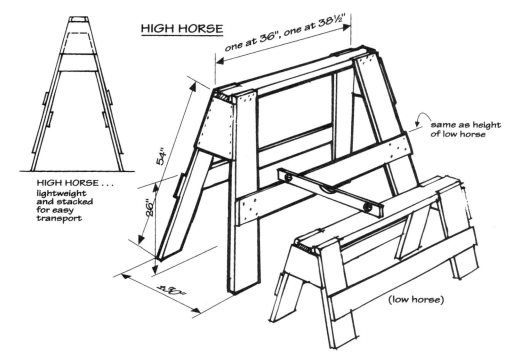

HIGH HORSE

one at 36", one at 38½"

same as height
of low horse

54"

36"

±30"

HIGH HORSE...
lightweight
and stacked
for easy
transport

(low horse)

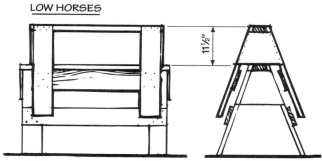

There are quite a few combinations in which these lightweight horses can be used.

LOW HORSES

11½"

36" long horse atop 40½" horse gives 11½" added height

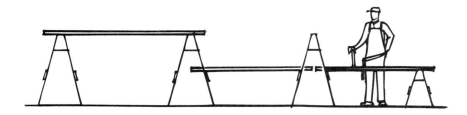

Radial Saw Stand and Doghouse Cover

This light-weight portable stand is for a Rockwell 10-inch contractor model saw. Adjust dimensions to fit others.

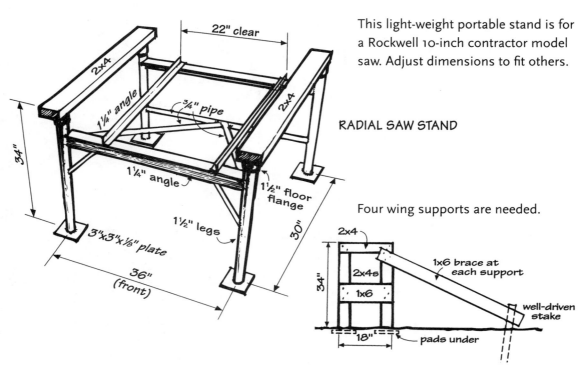

RADIAL SAW STAND

Four wing supports are needed.

After the stand is set up and wings are attached, eyeballed parallel to the saw's table fence, snap a parallel chalk line from end to end. Nail a 1 × 3 furring strip, on each wing, to this line. Be sure there is a gap between wings and saw's table to allow for doghouse cover. Make up a length (25 feet or so) of #10 wire, with a heavy-duty plug for the 220V connection to a work pole.

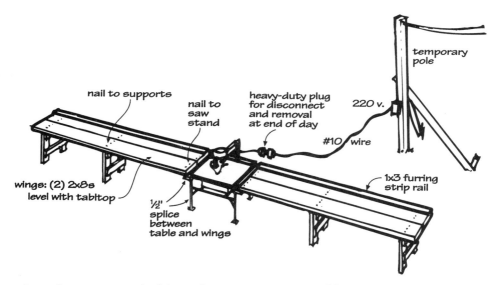

nail to supports

nail to saw stand

heavy-duty plug for disconnect and removal at end of day

220 v.

temporary pole

#10 wire

wings: (2) 2x8s level with tabltop

1x3 furring strip rail

½" splice between table and wings

Remove yoke with motor at end of day unless security is no problem.
A heavy-duty plug installed on the wire from the motor makes this easy.

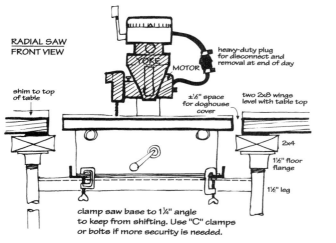

RADIAL SAW
FRONT VIEW

heavy-duty plug for disconnect and removal at end of day

shim to top of table

±½" space for doghouse cover

two 2x8 wings level with table top

YOKE

MOTOR

2x4

1½" floor flange

1½" leg

clamp saw base to 1¼" angle to keep from shifting. Use "C" clamps or bolts if more security is needed.

A doghouse cover for the radial saw keeps the elements away. A nail here and there will help secure it.

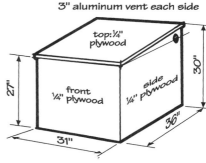

3" aluminum vent each side

top: ¼" plywood

side ¼" plywood

front ¼" plywood

27"

30"

31"

36"

glue with waterproof glue, then paint.

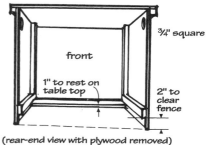

¾" square

front

1" to rest on table top

2" to clear fence

(rear-end view with plywood removed)

CHAPTER TWENTY-TWO

Ladder and Push Bracket

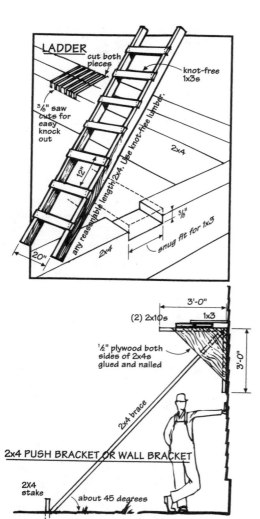

LADDER

cut both pieces

knot-free 1x3s

3/8" saw cuts for easy knock out

any reasonable length 2x4. Use knot-free lumber.

12"

2x4

2x4

3/8"

snug fit for 1x3

20"

One of the first things needed on a job is a ladder. Usually these ladders are 10 or 12 feet, but if a longer one is built, use straight-grained fir for greater strength. Mark and cut both rails at the same time. If you make two, cut all four at the same time.

3'-0"

(2) 2x10s   1x3

½" plywood both sides of 2x4s glued and nailed

3'-0"

2x4 brace

2x4 PUSH BRACKET OR WALL BRACKET

2X4 stake

about 45 degrees

Slip bracket over a long 2 × 4 and lean it against the building. Set up a matching one and then drive a stake at the base of each diagonal 2 × 4 brace. The brackets are now ready for the 2 × 10 planks.

CHAPTER TWENTY-THREE

"A" Frame Scaffolding

This scaffolding is cumbersome but effective. A good variation on this is to build just the top part 6 to 8 feet high. Although you can climb up the outside, it is better to use a ladder. Always put wood pads under scaffolding posts and legs to keep them from sinking into the ground.

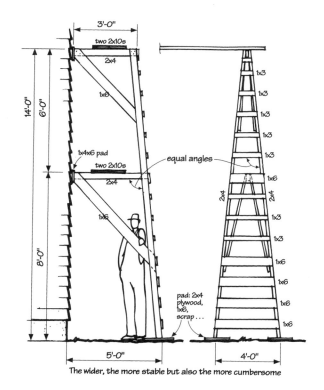

The wider, the more stable but also the more cumbersome

Tool Box

Tool boxes should have a place for nail sets, block plane, framing square, combination square, chisels, sharpening stone, oil can, hatchet, and level. The level should be protected in a separate compartment. The chisels and hatchet should have their edges protected. A separate box for handsaws is a must, and the blades must be separated from each other. A third catchall box for tools like hammers, nail picks, flat bars, screwdrivers, and wrenches is helpful. This box must be strong enough to handle the heavier weight but not too deep (to prevent piling up of too many tools).

There are many things one can do to keep tools from rattling around.

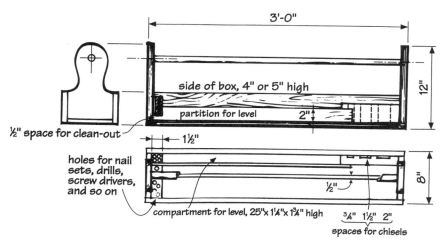

Rip all bottoms, ends, and inserts 5½ inches wide. Then rip all sides 5 inches wide, along with partitions as required. Sides and bottoms are all the same length. The handle is two end thicknesses less than the sides. The ends can be simple or fancy. The saw inserts will have to fit your saw lengths. The blades should be clear of the bottom; they stay sharper that way.

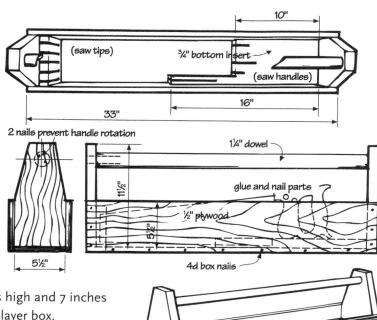

A shallow box 3½ inches high and 7 inches wide makes a good one-layer box.

Interior Finishing

Preparation

The exterior is finished. Now comes the interior.

Of course we timed it so that the bad weather will be spent doing the inside work.

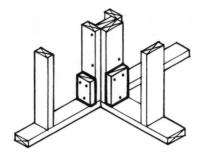

There is a lot of blocking to go in before the finished ceiling and finished walls go on.

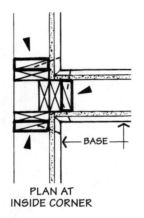

PLAN AT
INSIDE CORNER

The inside corners need blocking to make nailing the baseboard easier. You won't have to reach into the corner to find nailing.

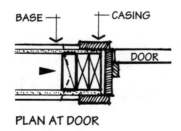

PLAN AT DOOR

Blocking at door openings is required for the same reason. The casing usually extends past the jamb studs, leaving very little to nail to.

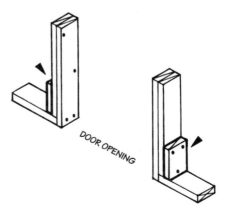

DOOR OPENING

Medicine cabinets are screwed to side blocking, so make sure there is something to screw into. The top and bottom should be blocked, too. It helps to mark the cabinet's location as the Sheetrock goes on; but even if unmarked, it is easy to locate.

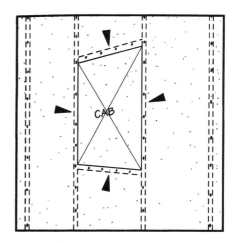

1 × 6 blocking is good enough for towel bars, shower heads, and faucets. It's a good idea to mark these locations on the Sheetrock.

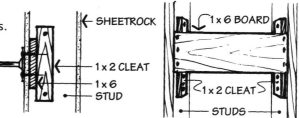

Paneling requires something more substantial.

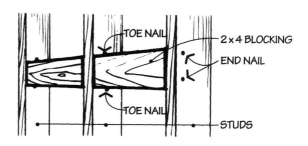

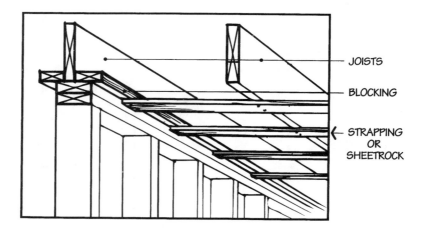

The ceiling should be prepared for either strapping or Sheetrock. Either way, it will need blocking.

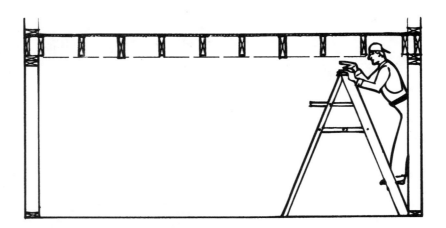

If the Sheetrock is to be installed directly on the joists, eyeball down to see if there are any low-hanging ones. If any need trimming, snap a chalk line and cut with a circular saw or hatchet.

If you can't cut it with a circular saw, a series of cuts across the bottom edge of the joist with a sharp hatchet . . .

. . . followed by strokes parallel to, and at, the chalk line will do a quick and neat job.

A "strongback" might be all that is needed to even up the bottoms, but not this kind of strong back.

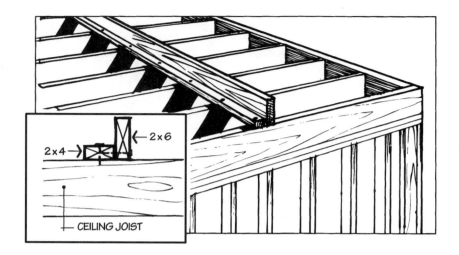

A strongback is a 2 × 6 nailed to a 2 × 4 and then nailed to the tops of the ceiling joists, pulling any bowed ones into line. A 2 × 8 can be used for more strength.

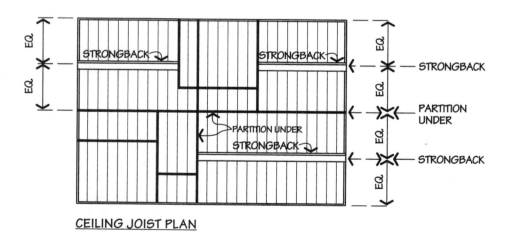

CEILING JOIST PLAN

The strongback is located at midspan and only where the floor space above the joists is not usable.

New England is the only place I know of that uses 1 × 3 strapping as a base for a Sheetrock ceiling. It is a terrific way to get a flat ceiling, but most carpenters just strap the ceiling and then install the Sheetrock without leveling it.

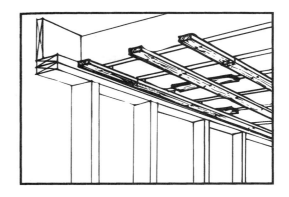

Eyeball for any bad joists and fix before strapping. The easiest way to get the job done is to nail up all the strapping and then eyeball for adjusting. For a super job, work to a stretched string.

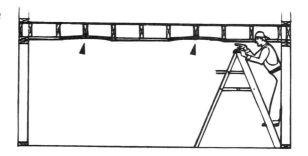

Use shingle tips, between strapping and joists, to adjust. I like to double-nail for a more stable condition, but a single nail will surely hold. When a ceiling needs joints in the strapping, alternate them.

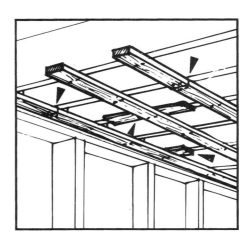

Measure the various size strapping lengths and cut them while the bundle is still tied together.

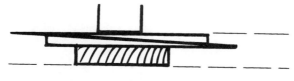

Two shingles used butt to tip makes a better shim job.

One shingle will tip the face. If the face is already tipped, then one shingle can correct it.

If plaster is to be used, then there is no need to worry about the joist bottoms; the plaster will take care of that. In the old days, the boss would encourage an apprentice to put on a thick coat of plaster by throwing a handful of sand into the skimpy coat already applied.

LET'S GET SOME PLASTER ON THERE, DAVE!!!

Check the walls for badly bowed studs by holding a long straight 2 × 4 against the wall. It will be obvious which ones are bad. A badly bowed stud in a finished wall really shows, so it is wise to replace or straighten it.

To straighten a bowed stud, cut well into it on the side opposite the hump.

The stud can then be pushed to a straight position. Wood-shingle tips driven into the cut will keep the stud straight while cleats are nailed on each side. It might take two such cuts if the bow is bad.

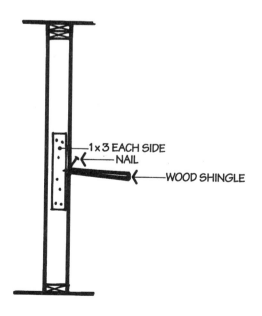

1 x 3 EACH SIDE
— NAIL
— WOOD SHINGLE

CHAPTER TWENTY-SIX

Insulation

Insulation plays a vital role in finishing a house, particularly in these days of high fuel costs. There are five problem areas that should be done with care: corners, partition intersections, roofs, spaces behind electrical-outlet boxes, and vapor barriers.

The standard outside corner does not insulate well.

VAPOR BARRIER

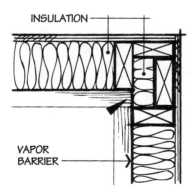

INSULATION

This corner allows for good insulation.

VAPOR BARRIER

If the "Finnish wall" (Scandinavian) is used and the 2 × 2s are planted on the face of the studs and parallel, insulate before the 2 × 2s go on in the corner. If the 2 × 2s are perpendicular to the studs, there is no problem.

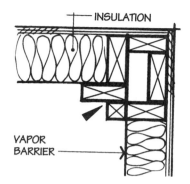

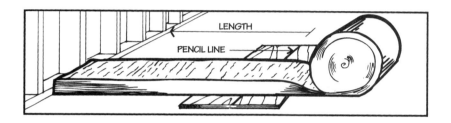

A pencil line on a piece of scrap plywood is a quick, easy guide for duplicate cutting of insulation. Position the plywood so that the pencil line indicates the length each strip of insulation is to be cut.

If there is a paper backing on the insulation, it should be down, with the fluff side up. Compress the insulation with a board that lines up with the pencil line and cut with a sharp utility knife.

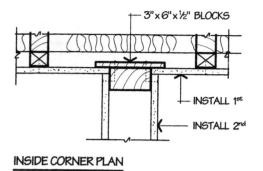

3" x 6" x ½" BLOCKS

INSTALL 1st

INSTALL 2nd

INSIDE CORNER PLAN

Where a partition butts an exterior wall, I favor Sheetrock clips or 3" × 6" × ½" plywood blocks at 16 inches on center. This allows for unbroken insulation between studs.

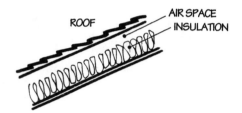

ROOF

AIR SPACE

INSULATION

There must be an air space between the top of the insulation and the bottom of the roofing boards to prevent condensation.

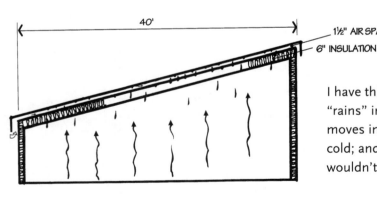

40'

1½" AIR SPACE

6" INSULATION

I have this condition in my house, and it "rains" inside because not enough air moves in the 40-foot roof. The roof is cold; and when the warm air hits it, you wouldn't believe the condensation.

An electrical-outlet box pretty much fills in a 2 × 4 stud wall. The result is that, directly behind the box, there is no insulation.

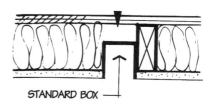

STANDARD BOX

The Finnish wall eliminates this problem by keeping the electrical work in the 1½-inch air space. This is not without its problems because of the shallow outlet boxes that must be used. The shallow box gets crowded in a hurry, but junction boxes will help.

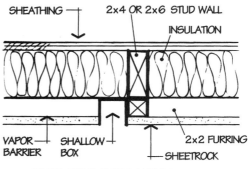

SHEATHING — 2x4 OR 2x6 STUD WALL
INSULATION

VAPOR BARRIER — SHALLOW BOX — 2x2 FURRING — SHEETROCK

THE FINNISH WALL

The Finnish wall also takes care of the vapor-barrier problem. Just 3 percent moisture in insulation reduces its "R" value by 50 percent; so the fewer breaks there are in the vapor barrier, the more efficient the insulation will be.

When sheets of polyethylene are joined, it is best to lock the seam for a good seal.

A basement wall is best insulated on the outside.

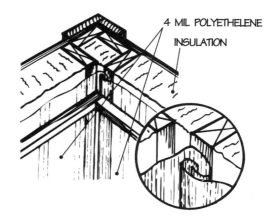

4 MIL POLYETHELENE
INSULATION

CHAPTER TWENTY-SEVEN

Underlayment

The kitchen and bathroom finished floors are usually vinyl over plywood underlayment. Versa-Board or any composition board is not a good product to use where there is moisture, since it swells when wet. Use plywood, plugged and sanded on one side; it's made for underlayment.

When kitchen or bathroom meets a hardwood floor, ⅝-inch plywood with ⅛-inch tile will make both floors about even.

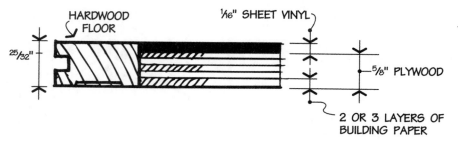

If ¹/₁₆-inch sheet of vinyl is used, a few layers of building paper will bring the vinyl surface flush with the hardwood. Try a sample of the plywood, building paper, and vinyl against a piece of flooring. Check the plywood; it's apt to measure anything these days.

With a door closed, the floor of the adjacent room should not be visible.

. . . door swings over vinyl floor

Door swings over wood floor . . .

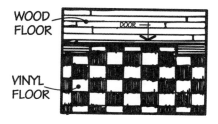

If the vinyl flooring extends around the door jambs, run the underlayment in one piece. There is a lot of traffic in these areas; and the more secure the underlayment is, the less wear there will be on the vinyl. Where the underlayment ends at a door, protect the edge with a piece of plywood nailed against it. It's temporary.

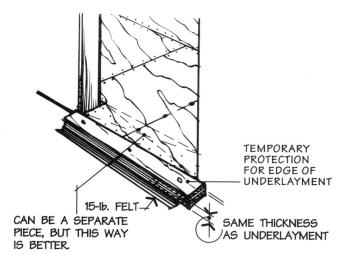

TEMPORARY PROTECTION FOR EDGE OF UNDERLAYMENT

15-lb. FELT CAN BE A SEPARATE PIECE, BUT THIS WAY IS BETTER.

SAME THICKNESS AS UNDERLAYMENT

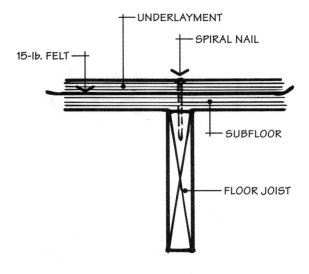

Snap a chalk line on the underlayment over every joist. The underlayment should be nailed through the subfloor into the joists for a secure floor. Use spiral flooring nails at the joists and ring shank nails in between and around the perimeter. If the underlayment has any movement, the nails want to walk out and push through the vinyl, so make sure it is securely nailed. For a really squeak-free floor, use mastic or construction adhesive, spread with a notched trowel, on the underlayment. The 15-lb. felt is not used with this system, but the same nailing is required.

RING SHANK NAIL

Both of these nails have good holding power.

SPIRAL FLOORING NAIL

Sheetrock

The ceiling is the place to start, and you need two people to do it. I have done the job alone, but I don't recommend it.

This guy is destined for disaster.

A couple of T-braces will make the job easier. Be sure you can reach them and still control the sheet overhead. It also helps to stick a few nails in the Sheetrock where the nailing will be. Holding the sheet overhead while fishing for nails can be tough.

The T-brace should be a little longer than the floor to ceiling height so that there is a slight wedge fit. If it is too long, the brace won't stay in place; if too short, the whole business comes down.

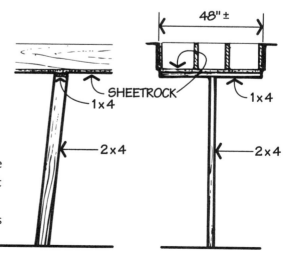

The easiest way to hold a sheet against the ceiling is with your head. The flatter the head, the better.

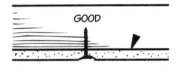

When nailing, make sure the sheet is pushed hard against the joists or strapping before driving the nail home.

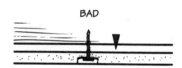

If you don't, the nail will pull through the surface of the Sheetrock.

If a nail misses a joist or stud, pull it out.

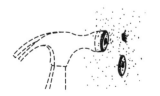

Hit the hole with a hammer hard enough to depress the surface without breaking the paper.

These dents, or dimples, can be filled easily with joint compound.

For a better, faster, and easier drywall hanging system, use drywall (Sheetrock) screws and a drywall screwdriver. The screwdrivers can be rented, cord or cordless, and are well worth the rental fee.

If the ceiling requires a butted joint at the end of a row, it should not land on a joist or strapping. The end is not tapered, and, when taped and spackled, it will show a bad bulge.

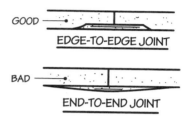

GOOD — EDGE-TO-EDGE JOINT

BAD — END-TO-END JOINT

One solution is to nail up blocking at 16 inches on center and then a 2 × 4 or strapping down the middle, parallel to the joists, so that the Sheetrock will be depressed ⅛ inch. The Sheetrock edges are then nailed or screwed to the 2 × 4 or strapping.

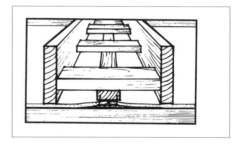

Another, more common, way is to cut four 12 × 12-inch squares of Sheetrock.

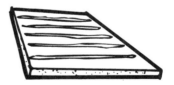

Butter these pieces with joint compound and slip them in on the back side of the panel already in place.

The next sheet is nailed in place and a piece of strapping is placed along the seam and held in place with cross pieces of strapping. These cross pieces will depress the joint, and the buttered 12 × 12s will dry holding everything in place. The joint is then taped and spackled like any other.

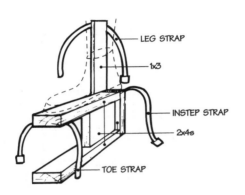

LEG STRAP

1x3

INSTEP STRAP

2x4s

TOE STRAP

Working from a ladder or horses is all right, but a simple pair of stilts can be a great help. I've heard that some places have outlawed their use because someone got hurt, so be cautious. I myself wouldn't try hanging sheet using stilts.

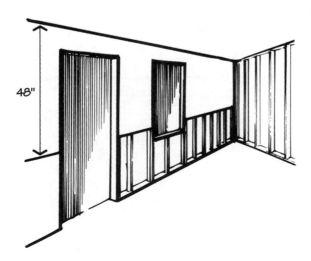

48"

Sheetrock walls are pretty simple. The panel that touches the ceiling should go in first to insure a good joint at the ceiling.

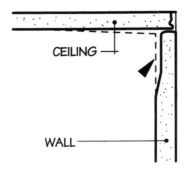

CEILING

WALL

Leave about a ½-inch gap at the floor so that a wedge can be slipped under to push the lower sheet up tight.

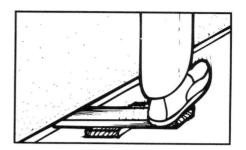

If corner clips or plywood blocks are used at inside corners, install the sheet that runs parallel to the blocks first; no nailing into these blocks or clips is required. The adjacent sheet is nailed to the stud in the corner and holds the first in place. Tape and spackle will keep the corner together.

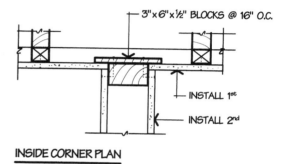

INSIDE CORNER PLAN

The only thing to remember about the outside corner is to make sure the Sheetrock extends far enough into the corner so that the corner bead will have backing behind it.

GOOD

Poor nailing condition here.

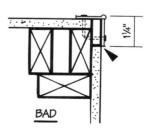

BAD

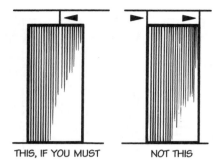

THIS, IF YOU MUST   NOT THIS

When Sheetrocking around doors and windows, run the sheet by in one piece and cut it out for the opening. If pieces are put in over the door or window, it will crack at the seam.

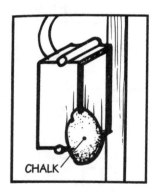

CHALK

Some professional Sheetrockers cover the wall and then cut the outlet and switch holes. A safer way is to rub the outlet box with block chalk, hold the sheet in place, smack it with an open palm, and cut the resulting mark left on the back side of the sheet. Another way is to measure the location and mark it on the sheet—not bad, but be prepared for a few mistakes.

A Stanley Surform is a good tool for shaving a Sheetrock edge. A piece of expanded wire lath wrapped around a block of wood, though, works just as well.

Don't forget to mark all openings for medicine cabinets, fans, and the like as the sheets go up. They are easily lost.

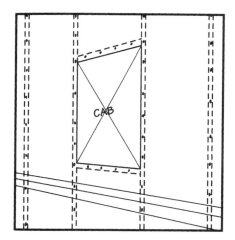

An aluminum "hawk" can be bought for around $15.00, but a plywood one will work almost as well and is a lot cheaper.

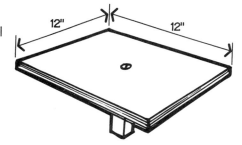

A 60-pound bucket of ready-mix joint compound is very convenient to work with. It's easy to scoop the compound out of.

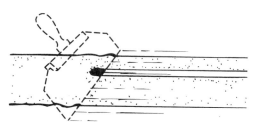

Cleanliness is a must. Any hard lumps or pieces of dirt will mess up a joint, so keep the cover on.

Load up the hawk by scooping compound from the bucket with a wood shingle. Keep the shingle in the bucket and cover to keep moist and clean.

Scrape the trowel clean as you work. If the scrapings are clean and soft, mix it with the stuff on the hawk. Try to keep the compound together so it won't dry out as fast. If there is any problem with it (hard lumps, dirt, etc.), dump it.

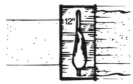 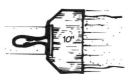 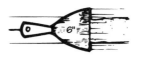 

Four trowels are required to do a good joint job: a 6-inch, 10-inch, and 12-inch, and a corner trowel.

To do a joint, start with a 6-inch trowel and put a layer of compound as wide as the tape the length of the joint.

The trowel held at a flattened angle will leave a nice bed of compound.

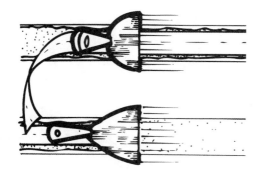

Lay the tape on the compound joint and push it flat with the 6-inch trowel. Get all the bubbles out.

Spread a thin layer of compound over the tape. Keep it smooth; you'll do less sanding that way.

Fiberglass tape with a sticky face eliminates the first step. You just stick it on and then apply a coat of compound. It's a big help when working overhead, but it costs about three times what paper tape does.

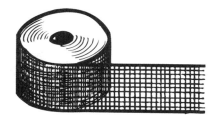

Raise the trowel toward perpendicular for smoothing. Try different angles for the best results.

The next coat is done the same way, but with the 10-inch trowel. That is, lay on a coat . . .

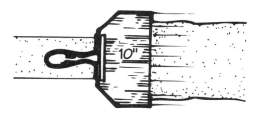

. . . wipe the trowel clean . . .

. . . then run the full length of the joint to smooth it out.

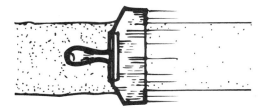

Every time the trowel is picked up from the joint, it pulls some compound with it, leaving a ridge; so try to do the joint in one stroke. Every bump the trowel hits reflects on the surface of the joint. When smoothing out, it may take a few strokes to get the excess off. Make that last stroke a nice one, since it's the base for the next coat.

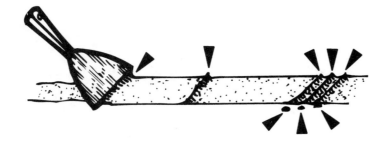

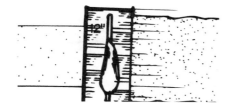

The last coat is done with the 12-inch trowel in the same manner as the others.

Try to make a long, smooth run for this coat.

The 12-inch trowel is much stiffer than the others and has a curved bottom, so it takes a good bit of pressure to smooth and feather out the final coat.

Each coat must be sanded when dry with 80 grit. Sand the last with 120 or finer. The better the joints are feathered, the less sanding will be required. Be sure to wear a good dust-filter mask while sanding.

A good place to use up the semidried compound is in nail holes and dents. Run the trowel at a flattened angle to leave a layer of compound in the dent.

Then hold the trowel almost perpendicular, apply enough pressure to bend its blade, and scrape the surface flat. Go to the next dent, deposit, scrape, next, deposit, and scrape; to the next, deposit, and scrape; and so on.

Inside corners are done in a similar fashion, but here the paper tape is prefolded to fit the corner. The tape has a crease down the middle, so folding is easy. There are folding tools available.

The procedure is the same, but use the corner trowel to lay in the first coat of compound . . .

. . . lay in the tape . . .

. . . a coat of compound, and sand. Then smooth on a finish coat of compound.

Exterior corners are the easiest of all. Nail on the metal corner bead and compound the joints with the 6-inch trowel.

There will be excess compound running around the corner as you trowel, but not to worry. It's easy to scrape and sand the metal corner.

CHAPTER TWENTY-FIVE

Paneling

If a wall is to be covered with plywood panel sheets, the best installation is over ⅜-inch Sheetrock. It's solid and makes for better sound proofing.

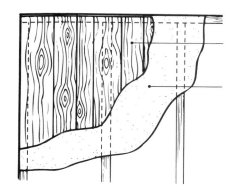

The next best way is on horizontal strapping (16 inches on center).

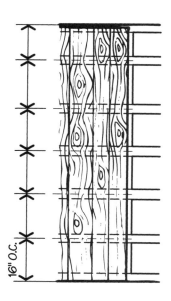

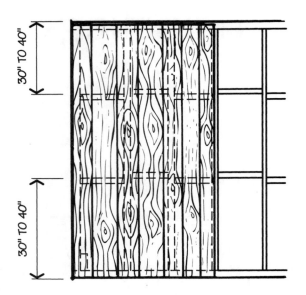

If applied directly to studs, block the studs at 30 to 40 inches from top and bottom.

This will protect the areas where bumping occurs.

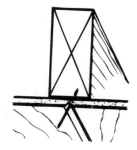

When nailing in the V-groove, nail through the side of the V at a slight angle; it holds better.

With any trim, look for ways to hide joints. With paneling, the last piece is the toughest to fit, so look for a good place to hide it. A door or window near a corner is a good place to make that last joint.

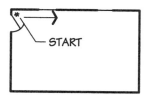

With solid ³/₄-inch paneling laid up vertically, 2 × 4 horizontal blocking is needed. If the blocks are put in flat and staggered, they are easier to nail, and it leaves a straight line of wood to nail into. You don't have to guess where the nailing is.

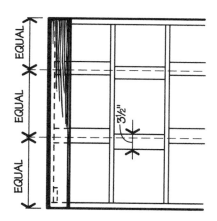

Before any paneling is nailed up, it is a good idea to spread it around the room so it can be looked over. Match the paneling, look for very dark or light; pick out odd-looking ones. Cut up those that don't blend in and use them for trim.

Back prime if there is a moisture problem.

If the panels are to be painted or stained dark, it is a good idea to paint the tongues so they won't show when the boards shrink.

The joints don't always stay like this.

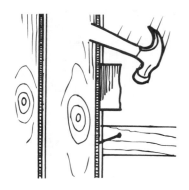

Use a scrap piece of paneling (the groove edge) as a block to hammer against and drive each panel up tight.

Start in a corner that will make the last piece easy to install.

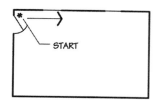

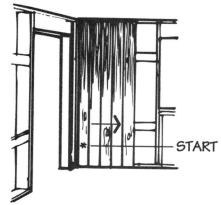

START

Plumb and, if necessary, scribe the first board to fit the corner. Toenail just above the tongue at the blocking and set these nails. Face nail at the top and bottom where the base and molding will cover nails.

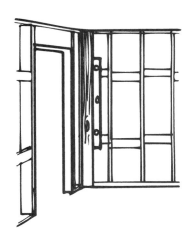

There is no great mystery to nailing each panel, but do check the plumb once in a while and adjust.

To aid in driving a stubborn board over, start a nail with the tongue edge of a panel raised slightly.

PLUMB

PLUMB

Inside corners will have to be scribed with the board held in the plumb position.

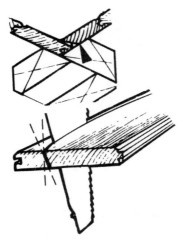

Rip with a handsaw and back-cutting for a tight fit in front.

The outside corner is mitered and relieved at the back of the miter so that the front of the miter will be tight.

If the next to the last piece of panel at an outside corner is plumb (and it should be), take the longest measurement to the corner and use it for a parallel 45-degree-plus cut on the table saw. If the corner is badly out of plumb, it will have to be measured top and bottom for this cut.

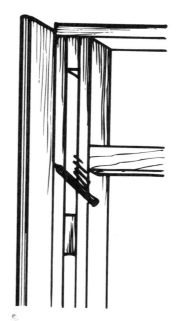

Transfer the marks on the back to the front with a 45-degree combination square and rip with a handsaw.

A sharp ripsaw does this job nicely.

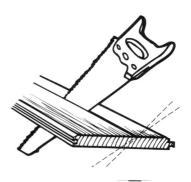

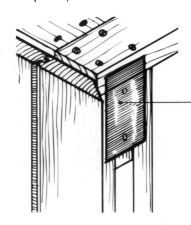

BUILDING PAPER FOR SHIMMING

If an outside corner isn't perfect, a little fudging can be done with building-paper shims.

For an inside corner, the last space is measured top and bottom.

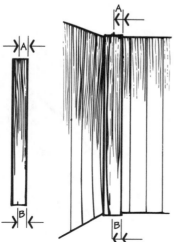

Mark the panel, tack in place parallel to the next-to-last board, and scribe.

This scribed line is ripped with a sharp ripsaw. Be sure to back-cut it.

When working with paneling, be extra careful about keeping hands clean. It's easier than cleaning the paneling.

CHAPTER THIRTY

Door Frames

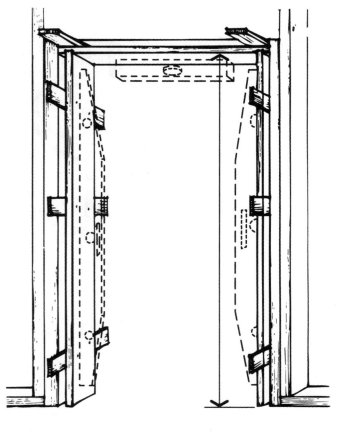

More real finish work: door frames. There are two things to consider here: style and width.

For style, there are two choices, rabbeted and planted-on stop. I prefer the planted stop because it helps overcome many door problems.

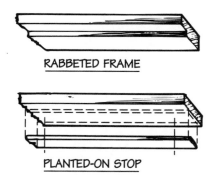

RABBETED FRAME

PLANTED-ON STOP

If the door is warped, the stops are planted to allow the door to hit all around. The same can be done if the jambs are not parallel. The door is hung, and then the stops are planted on the frame to hit the door. Simple.

With the rabbeted frame you are pretty much stuck with these problems.

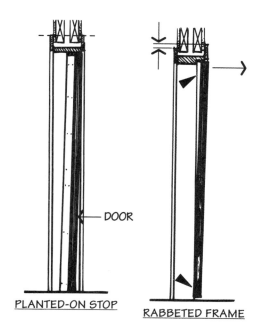

DOOR

PLANTED-ON STOP

RABBETED FRAME

Another good reason for the planted-on stop is that, on both sides of the door, the head casings will always be at the same level.

Not so with the rabbeted frame.

The inside is higher than the outside with the rabbeted frame.

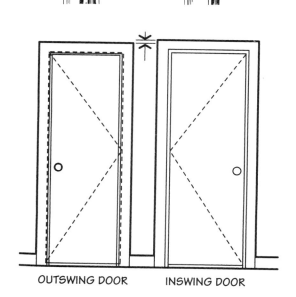

OUTSWING DOOR

INSWING DOOR

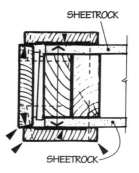

The width is decided by measuring from face of Sheetrock to face of Sheetrock at the door openings. You will be surprised at the variations, not only from door to door, but also top to bottom and side to side. Of course, the more carefully the framing was done, the fewer the problems like this that will occur. A good framer is worth two finish men.

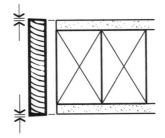

The frames should be a tad wider than the measurement decided on and beveled back on both edges.

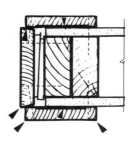

This will allow for a good joint between the casing and the frame. A sharp planer blade on a table saw does a good job. As the pieces are beveled, mark the inside face so that the right face will be grooved for the head frame and the frame will be assembled properly.

There is also a choice when putting frames together. Either groove out the jambs to receive the header . . .

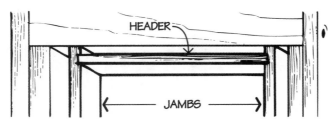

. . . or groove out the header to receive the jambs. I prefer to groove the header; it's more stable in the rough opening.

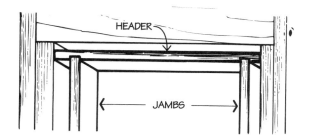

Square up head and jamb with a framing square.

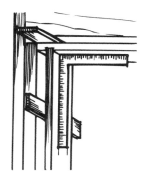

Square frame to partition with framing square.

It's a good idea to cut all the headers and jambs for the frames at the same time. Cut them a little longer than required and trim to fit later. The jambs will all be the same length: the door height plus the depth of the groove in the header, header clearance, threshold clearance, and finished-floor thickness. The headers should be at least 1 inch longer than the rough-opening width and cut to fit after assembly.

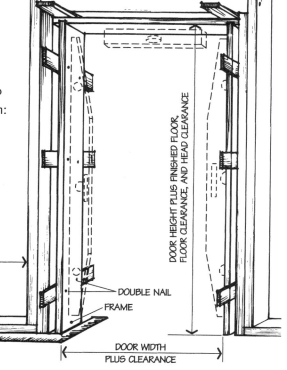

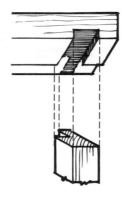

The grooves in the header are best cut with a dado blade on the table saw, but a knife, handsaw, and chisel will do a fine job.

Start from the center of the header and mark right and left one-half the door width plus the clearance required.

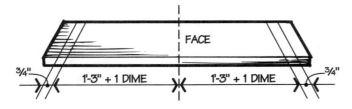

FACE

3/4"   1'-3" + 1 DIME   1'-3" + 1 DIME   3/4"

FOR A 2'-6' DOOR

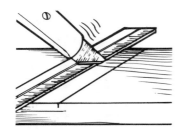

If it is a handsaw-and-chisel job, start by scoring with a sharp knife along a combination square before cutting with a sharp finish saw. This will give a nice, clean, positive line. Cut both sides of the groove only as deep as required (about ¼ inch) before chiseling.

Use the finished header as a pattern for making duplicate headers. There's less chance for error that way.

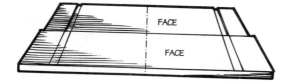

FACE

FACE

Before grooving and assembling, check for what face goes where; it's easy to mess up here.

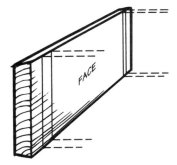

With the frame assembled, cut the header for a tight fit in the rough opening.

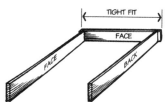

Slip the whole business into the opening and level the header by shimming the bottoms of the jambs. Once it is leveled, snug it down by wedging shingle tips directly over the jambs.

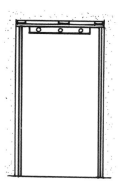

Shim the bottom side of one jamb until plumb using a jamb level (a great tool for door work). A regular six-foot level will work. Then shim the middle to a straight line.

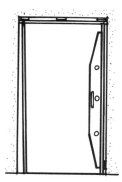

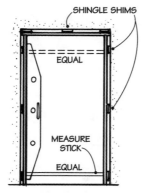

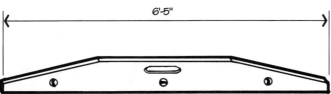

The opposite jamb can then be shimmed over parallel by using a cut-to-size measuring stick.

This door-jamb level is also a straightedge.

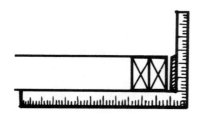

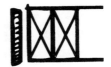

When shimming with shingles, use two opposing each other except when the framing behind is twisted. In such cases you might need two in the same direction to make the trim piece come square with the work.

Use a framing square at the base of the opening to square the jamb frame with the wall.

Make sure that the header is square with the jamb.

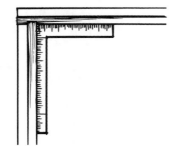

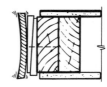

Always double-nail the jambs to prevent warping and to make a more secure fastening. Nailing up the middle merely holds the piece in place; it does not securely fasten it.

Doors

If the doors haven't been prehung, now is the time to hang them. There should be good clearance on each side, top, and bottom:

about one dime's thickness at the top and sides if the door is to be stained,

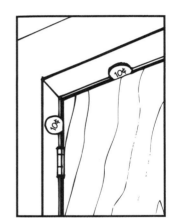

about one nickel's thickness at the top and sides if the door is to be painted,

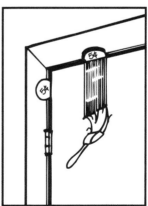

one-eighth inch plus the finished floor and threshold if one is to be used.

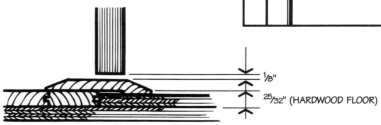

1/8"

25/32" (HARDWOOD FLOOR)

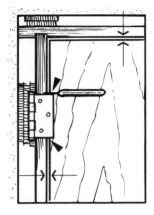

If all is square and plumb, the door should fit with no trouble. Some temporary stop pieces will hold the door in place while marking the butt locations. Shim the door to the proper height and mark the jamb and door with a sharp knife.

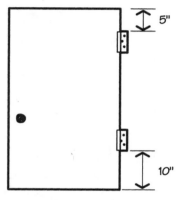

WOOLWORTH'S 5 AND 10

The door butts (hinges) are usually set at 5 inches and 10 inches. I always think of Woolworth's 5 & 10 Store as a reminder.

A door jack is a great help when working on doors. Some carpenters use two 2 × 4 × 32 feet, but I find the second one a foot tripper. The jack simply supports the door in a solid vertical position.

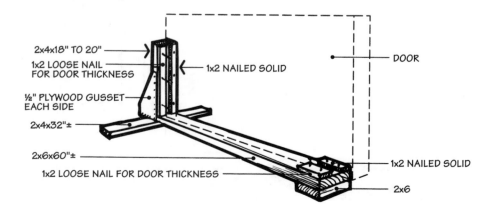

2x4x18" TO 20"

1x2 LOOSE NAIL FOR DOOR THICKNESS

1x2 NAILED SOLID

½" PLYWOOD GUSSET EACH SIDE

2x4x32"±

2x6x60"±

1x2 LOOSE NAIL FOR DOOR THICKNESS

DOOR

1x2 NAILED SOLID

2x6

Hinge binding, a big problem with doors, can easily be avoided if enough clearance is left between the doorstop and the door.

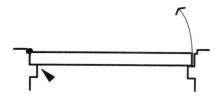

If the door is hinge-bound, the hinge must be moved away from the stop or the stop moved away from the door.

If the hinge is moved back, a wood shim should be laid in to fill the gap and to keep the hinge in place.

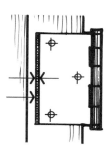

If a door is not plumb, it will either want to open by itself or stay closed.

OPEN SESAME

LATCH EDGE

Cardboard shims behind the hinge will change the hang of the door. Shim the top hinge to lower the latch edge, shim the bottom hinge to raise the latch edge.

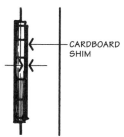

CARDBOARD SHIM

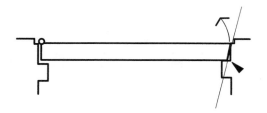

The latch side of a door should be beveled to allow for clearance as the door swings past the stop.

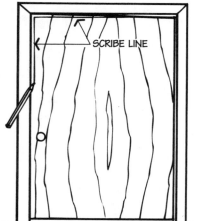

In a "door jack," the door is easy to work on.

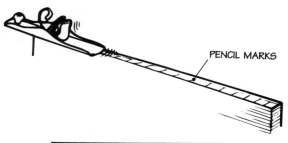

PENCIL MARKS

When planing a bevel on a door, a series of pencil marks across the edge will show how the bevel is progressing. A final check is made with a combination square.

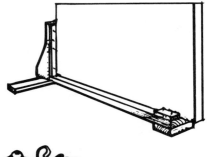

SCRIBE LINE

If the door has proper clearance on the hinge side and hits the header or the opposite jamb, the door must be planed to fit. Close the door as far as it will go and scribe with a pencil, allowing for clearance. Pull the hinge pins, put the door in the door jack, and plane it down.

For setting locks, borrow or rent a lock-boring kit that is made for the lockset being installed. Lumber yards have these. Otherwise, it's measure and drill with a brace and bit.

I have put a lot of hinges on with a combination square, a sharp knife, and a sharp chisel.

The outline is cut to the depth of the hinge.

The depth is marked on the face of the door for the length of the hinge.

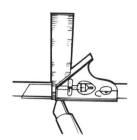

A series of chisel strokes will rough it out.

With the chisel held flat, the job is finished off. When I work a chisel with my hands, I work with restraint. One hand guides while the other pushes. A sharp tool can be controlled easier than a dull one.

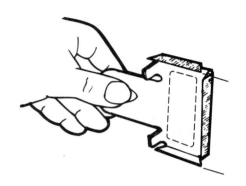

Stanley makes a butt-marking tool that combines all three steps in one tool. One arm sets for the width, the other for the depth. This scribing tool has sharp edges for cutting the outline, like the knife and square setup. The chisel work is still required.

Stanley also makes a butt marker that is put in place and hit with a hammer. The sharp edges leave the outline ready for chiseling. It comes in many sizes.

All these tools are good, but the very best system for doing many doors is the router and butt template guide. Once set up, jambs and doors are routed quickly and accurately. The guide is expensive and cannot be rented.

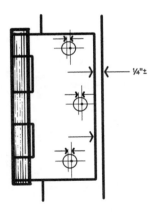

Butts are set with the edge about ¼ inch from the face of the door, and the screws are offset in the holes to force the butt against this edge.

Door Casing

Now for some exciting finish work: casings. Mark the reveal on the edge of the frames with a combination square as a guide. Better still, make up a marking gauge from a piece of ³/₄-inch pine. The combination square is apt to slip, making some funny-looking reveals.

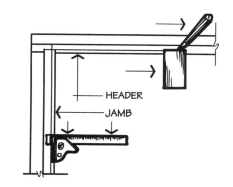

WINDOW OR DOOR FRAME

The wood gauge is always the same, and it frees the combination square for other jobs. The usual reveal is about ¼ inch, but suit yourself.

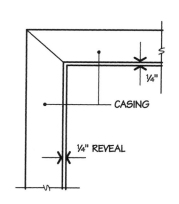

¼" REVEAL

CASING

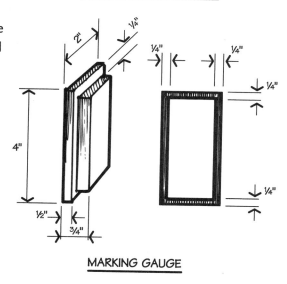

MARKING GAUGE

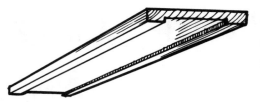

The two basic choices with casings are mitered and square corners, and they are more easily fitted if the backs are relieved.

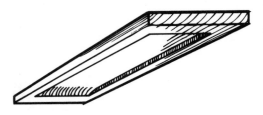

This is particularly helpful on bad walls. If square corner casings are used, they cannot be relieved to the ends because they show (unless the corners are mitered).

The easiest way to relieve the casings is with a dado blade on a table saw. The mitered casings are run right through, but the square ones are started short and ended short.

The best tool for trim work is an electric miter box. You can't beat it for speed and accuracy. If a thin shaving is required, there is no better way than with this tool.

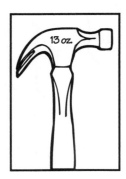

Most carpenters carry one 16-ounce hammer, and it will do for any and all jobs, even fine finish work. Still, I prefer a 13-ounce for finish work; the control is so much better. These hammers are not so easy to find these days, but the best supply houses will carry them.

If the casings go on before the floor, slip a loose piece of flooring under the casing before any measurements are taken. Square the bottom of the side casings by holding them against the reveal line and scribing to the floor.

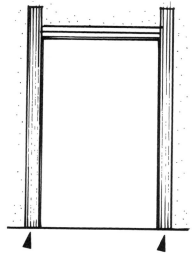

Start on one side casing and mark the height with a sharp knife at the reveal line on the head frame.

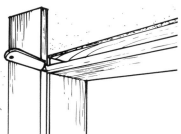

If the head and jamb are square then, for a square casing (non-mitered), a square cut at the top of the side casing will work. If they are not square, then a trial cut, a little longer than the reveal mark, is made, and a trial fit with the head casing follows. When the trial fit is right, repeat it at the proper length on the side casing. Tack it in place.

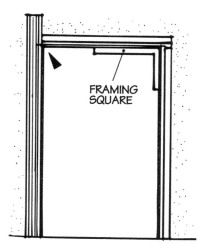

FRAMING SQUARE

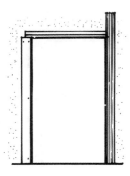

Repeat for the other side casing.

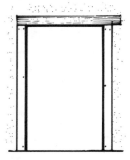

Square-cut one end of the head casing, hold in place, and mark with a sharp knife. Cut and hold in place to check the fit.

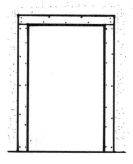

The finished product.

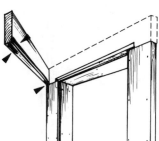

Before nailing in place, I like to run a bead of glue on the back of the casing where it touches the frame and where the header sits on the side casings. Be careful if the wood is to be stained, because stain will not take on a glued surface.

You can, of course, cut all the pieces to the right lengths, nail, sand, and fill the gaps, and it might look all right. But if the trim is to be stained, it never will look good unless you custom-fit each casing.

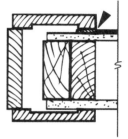

If there is bad framing at the opening, it can be overcome by shimming or shaving the back of the casing. Here is where the relieving on the backside of the casings helps.

If the head casing tips back . . .

. . . a wedge-shaped shim will make it right. It is always best when the face of the casings are on the same plane.

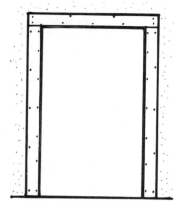

Use 8d finish or casing nails at the outer edge and 4d or 6d at the inner edge. Use as many nails as are required to fasten the trim securely in place.

Rap the trim with the knuckles and listen for the telltale rattle of looseness. Also nail wherever the trim is pulling away from the wall or frame.

If a piece of trim must be pulled and used again, don't drive the nails out. Pull them through to keep the face clean.

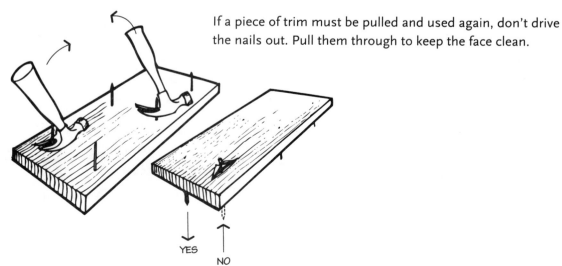

The mitered casing is started the same way as the square casing: by marking the reveal line on the frame.

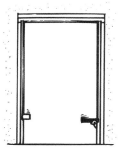

The side casing sits on the finished floor, or blocks simulating the finished floor, and is scribed to fit.

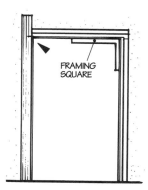

Make sure the header is square with the jamb, and mark the header reveal line on one side casing.

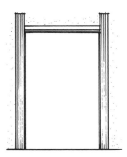

FRAMING SQUARE

If all is square, then a 45 degree cut is made and the casing is tacked in place.

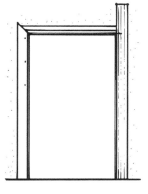

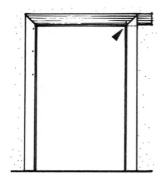

Cut a 45-degree angle on a piece of header stock. Hold in place and, if it needs correcting, shave it with the miter box or a sharp block plane. Hold the trim piece securely while planing; you make cleaner cuts that way. When the fit is good, mark for length at the side-frame reveal line.

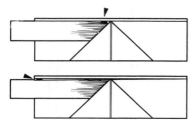

Put wedges of whatever thickness at the right or left end of the piece of trim in the miter box to get the desired angle.

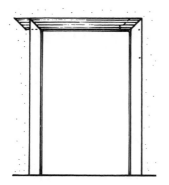

Make a trial cut past the mark and see how it fits. When the fit is good, duplicate the cut at the correct length.

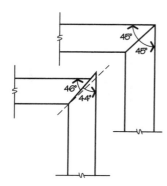

A mitered joint must be made up of pieces cut on equal angles or you get an odd corner. You can fudge a little, though, especially if the trim is to be painted.

If the header is tipped back, the miter will be open at the face.

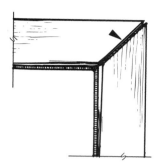

If it is not too bad, it can be corrected by raising (shimming) the piece in the miter box at the saw-blade end. This will relieve the back edge of the miter. Glue it the same as the square casing, including the miter.

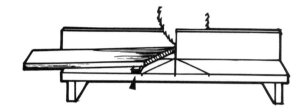

Nail the trim securely and test by knocking.

The telltale "clack clack" needs nailing.

If the trim is to be painted, sand the joints with a piece of sandpaper wrapped around a block of wood while the glue is still wet. A better tool is a small random orbital sander. The dust will fill in nicely, making an invisible joint. Stained work must fit without sanding because every scratch will show after staining.

Window Casing

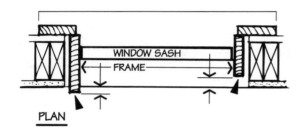

PLAN

Window casing is basically similar to door casing. The window frame has to be packed out or planed back to the interior-wall face.

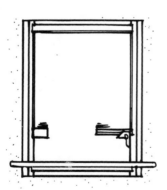

Then, if there is a reveal, it is marked on the frame.

The stool is then scribed to fit against the wall and window, with a little bit of gap at the window to allow for paint and window clearance ($1/32$ inch minimum).

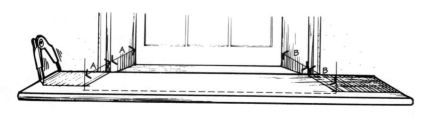

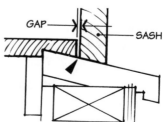

The stool length will be about ³/₄ inch past the side casings, so keep the rough piece plenty long. The stool piece might have to be ripped to extend no more than ³/₄ inch past the face of the casing and apron.

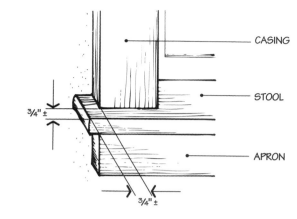

The cut parallel to the jamb is marked.

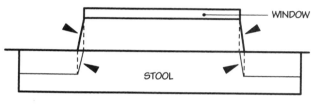

Cut the two notches and tack the stool in place.

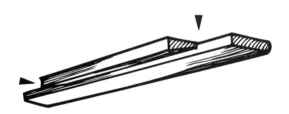

Now the side casings are cut on the bottoms to fit the stool. They should be square cuts. The top cuts are marked . . .

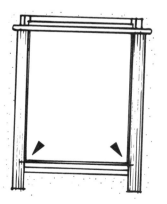

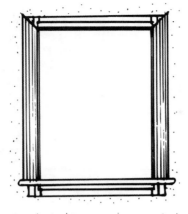

. . . and cut.

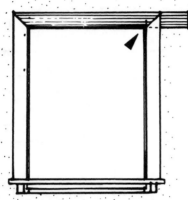

One side casing is tacked in place, and a trial header end is cut and fitted. The opposite end is marked for length.

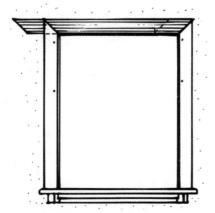

The other end is trial cut and fitted.

The stool is nailed in place first, then the casings. It's a good idea to prime the underside of the stool, which sits on the windowsill. Drive a nail from the bottom of the stool up into each of the side casings.

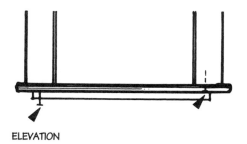

ELEVATION

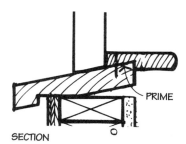

PRIME

SECTION

The apron reaches from outside of casing to outside of casing.

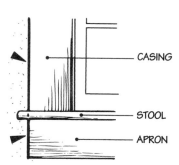

CASING

STOOL

APRON

If trim is stained, cut a 45-degree return at each end of the apron. End grain stains darker than face grain.

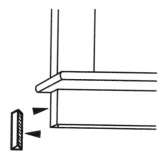

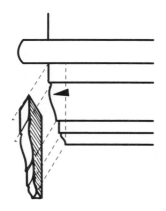

If the trim is molded, shape the return with a coping saw when trim is to be painted. Otherwise, a 45-degree return piece should be fitted.

Nail the apron in place, making sure the stool is square with the window.

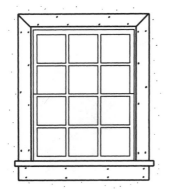

The finished product.

A neat piece of equipment to use for casing work is the "cricket." It's light, the right height, and stable; and it has a shelf for carrying tools and things around on. More on this tidbit later.

Baseboard

When putting in baseboard or ceiling trim, keep in mind what you see when entering a room and make the joints in such a way that they look good no matter how bad they might be. In this case the joints on both sides of the room are bad, but the joints on the right are obvious and the ones on the left are not.

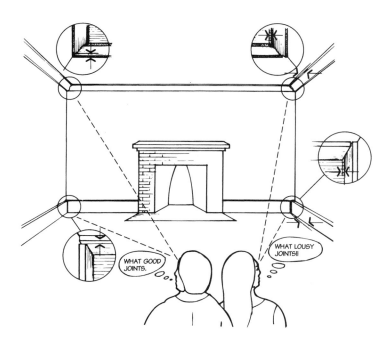

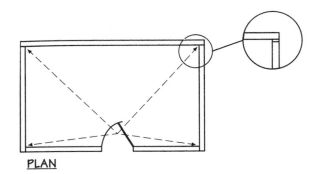

If the piece on the wall opposite the door goes in first, the seam of the joint will be to the side and hard to see.

PLAN

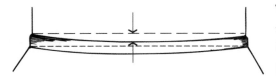

The best joint is a coped joint. There is a buildup of joint compound in the corners, so they are rarely square. The coped corner, when snapped in place, is a very tight fit.

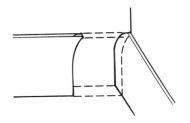

With the coped corner, the first piece in is cut square on each end and a tad long. The piece is bowed away from the wall at the center and pushed into place at the ends. If the piece is the right length, it will gently snap from your hand when the center is moved closer to the wall. If it is too long, it just won't go at all; if it is a little (as opposed to a tad) too long, the Sheetrock corner will crack.

The next piece is cut at a 45-degree angle as if it were a mitered corner. Rub a pencil on the front corner of this miter so that it will be easier to follow with the coping saw (hence the "coped corner").

Start the coping saw on the top, at 90 degrees or perpendicular to the back and, as you follow the penciled corner, ease the saw back from perpendicular to about 87 degrees. Or start on the bottom at 87 degrees and work toward the top, easing over to 90 degrees.

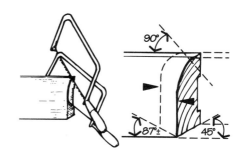

This will ensure that the front edge will hit hard against the adjacent piece of baseboard. Measure from the face of the baseboard already in place to the opposite wall and mark this on the coped piece. Add a little to make a snap fit. It's really simple, but it might take a few practice cuts to get the hang of it.

Even intricate molding shapes can be cut this way. Ceiling molding is done the same way.

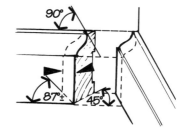

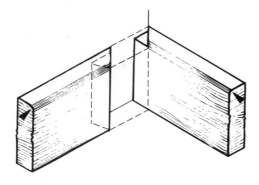

The best-looking corner for square base is the combination mitered-and-coped joint. This square base usually has a rounded upper corner.

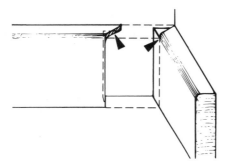

The first piece is square cut and then mitered for about ⅛ inch at the top (to the bottom of the round corner). The adjacent piece is mitered and then cut, from the bottom, up to the bottom of the round corner. Back-cut for a tight fit in front. Cut across with a knife, and there remains about a ⅛-inch miter lip.

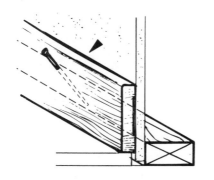

Baseboard is nailed at the studs, top and bottom. Sometimes the base is not tight against the wall between studs, but we shall overcome. Use 16d finish nails high on the base and angle down to reach the 2 × 4 plate. When the nail is set, it should pull the base in.

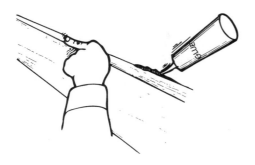

If there is still a space between base and wall, squeeze some glue in and smooth with a finger. It might take a few coats. Don't use this method if the trim is to be stained.

When a "duck puddle" is created with a poorly aimed hammer, just put a dab of saliva in the dent, a double dab if the dent is deep. (If you are chewing tobacco, use a friend.)

Drill . . . nail . . . set.

If the trim is hardwood, predrilling the nail holes is a must. A good drill bit is a nail of the size being used to nail the trim. Cut the head off and sharpen the point.

There should never be a shortage of drill bits of any size as long as there is a piece of stiff wire around. Big nails, little nails, welding rod—anything will do. Beat on the end to flatten and flair, then file cutting tips.

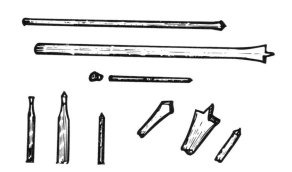

If you want a nail to slide into wood a little easier, rub it in your hair to pick up the oil.

Face oil works, too.

It acts like wax or soap on a wood screw.

Saliva on a wood screw will help if soap is not available.

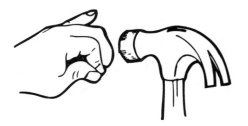

When nailing thin brads, squeeze the brad with the fingers; it won't bend so easily.

Fitting a Shelf

You can't just cut a board square at each end and expect it to fit in a corner. The joint compound buildup changes the angle in the corner, so it should be scribed.

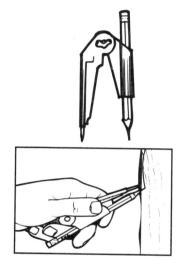

The scribe tool is just a small compass that locks at any position desired.

Set the scribe to the desired spacing and run the metal point along the wall. The pencil makes a parallel line.

Measuring for a shelf in a closet is easy with a folding rule that has a sliding inset at one or both ends.

Another tool for in-between measuring is this slipstick, which is made from a matched pair of tongue-and-groove sticks.

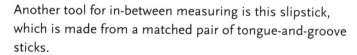

SECTION

Both tools are used the same way. The rule has one advantage; you can read a number, and, if it slips, it can be reset to that number. The rule, though, unlike the slipstick, is limited to six feet.

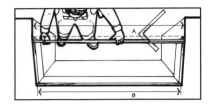

Use the folding rule or slipstick to find the longest dimension.

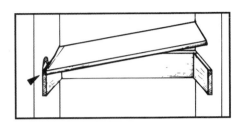

Cut the board a little longer than the longest dimension, put it in place tipped up at one end, and scribe. The scribe should be set to hit the corner of the edge, where there is space between the board and the wall.

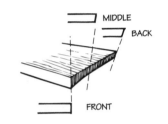

Cut this line, starting square at the front and back-cutting as you progress. Test this cut against the wall and correct with a block plane if necessary.

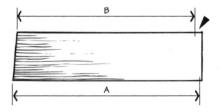

Measure the opening, front "A" and back "B," and transfer them to the shelf board.

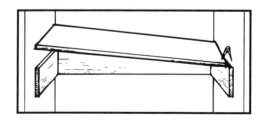

Slip the shelf in place, tipped up at the other end, and scribe. The scribe should be set to hit one of the marks on the board and, when scribed, should hit the other mark. Cut this end the same way the other end was cut, and it should be a perfect fit. A little block planing might be in order. With the shelf in place, scribe and fit to the back wall.

Stairs

Although the frame work of stairs is not inside finish work, it ties in so closely that I have to include it here.

The use of the calculator makes the mathematics of this job easy. To begin with, choose fourteen risers (about an average number), and divide that number into the floor-to-floor height (108 inches in this case). 108 inches divided by 14 = 7.71-inch riser.

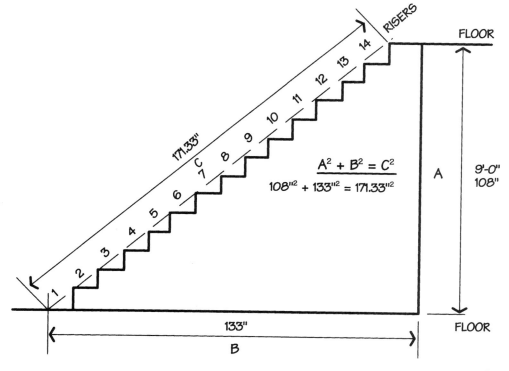

$$A^2 + B^2 = C^2$$
$$108^{"2} + 133^{"2} = 171.33^{"2}$$

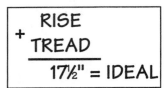

The ideal rise plus tread total is 17½ inches

17.50" ideal total
less . . . . 7.71" the riser we came up with
equals . . . . . . 9.79" our ideal tread
(for this example)
— use . . . . . . 9.50" a stock tread size
times . . . . .14 tread spaces
equals . . . . . 133"

From school, we remember A² + B² = C²; so
108² + 133² = 171.3²

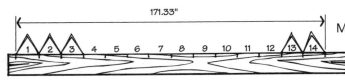

Mark this dimension on a 15-foot 2 × 12. It will fit on a 14-footer, but the ends are usually split and may have other bad spots we would like to avoid. This 171.33 inches will have to be divided into the fourteen equal tread spaces with a pair of large dividers.

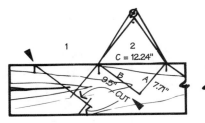

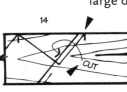

Write "cut" on the carriage so you know what line to cut.

$$A^2 + B^2 = C^2$$
$$7.71^{112} + 9.5^{112} = 12.24^{112}$$

The easiest way to find this spacing dimension is with the same A² + B² = C² formula.

Set the dividers and walk them up the 2 × 12. With luck you will hit the 171.33-inch mark. Keep adjusting the dividers until you go from mark to mark fourteen times.

Mark the fourteen spaces clearly. Then set up a framing square with the rise and tread dimensions by clamping a 2 × 4 across it.

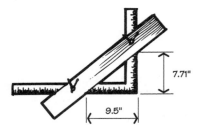

Start at either end and outline the rise and tread at each mark.

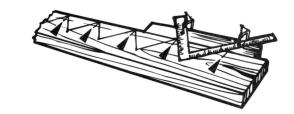

Mark the bottom of this carriage for whatever framing condition exists.

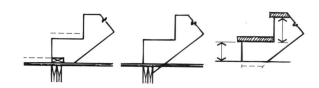

Mark the top of the carriage for the framing condition. Don't forget to take the finished floor into account on both top and bottom.

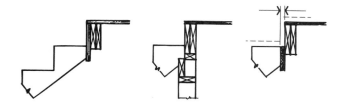

The carriage layout will look like this.

Double-check the layout before cutting. When satisfied, cut freehand with a power saw or handsaw. Run the cuts a little past where they intersect so that the triangles will fall out. We can use these later.

Now the carriage looks like this.

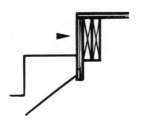

Try it in place and don't forget the 3/4-inch hanger board if one is to be used.

Three carriages are usually required, so use the completed carriage as a pattern for the other 2 × 12s. A 2 × 6 with the triangular cutout blocks nailed on can be used for the middle carriage.

The middle carriage with blocks will look like this.

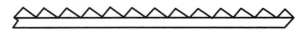

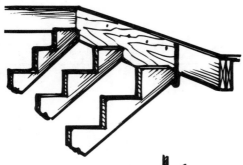

If a hanger board is used, nail the carriages to it and then nail the whole business in place.

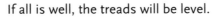

If all is well, the treads will be level.

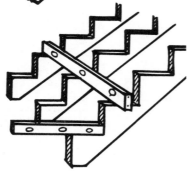

For let-in treads with no risers, the basic layout is the same.

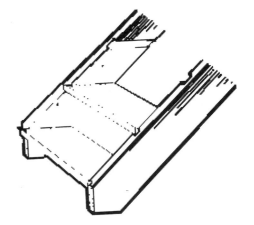

The grooves for the trades (usually 2 × 10) are made with a series of parallel cuts with a power saw set to the proper depth. Break away the pieces in the groove and clean up with a chisel.

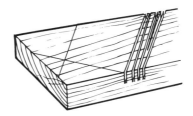

Here is the finished product.

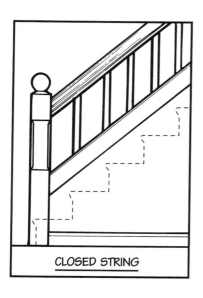

CLOSED STRING

Finishing a stairway is a measure-twice-cut-once, precision piece of carpentry. The first house I built has my first stairway, so it is not impossible even for a beginner. There are two types of stairways: the closed string and the open string.

2'-6" TO 2'-8"

OPEN STRING

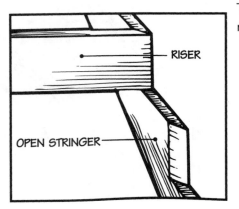

This is an open string or stringer, mitered to receive the riser.

Combination open and closed stringer—very common.

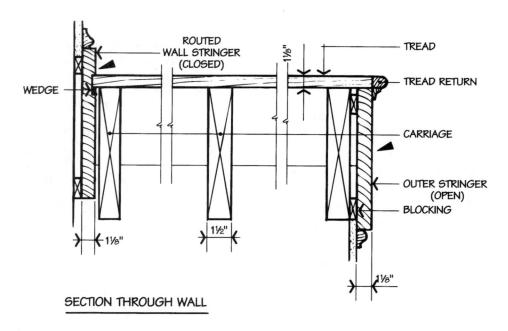

SECTION THROUGH WALL

This is a routed closed stringer.

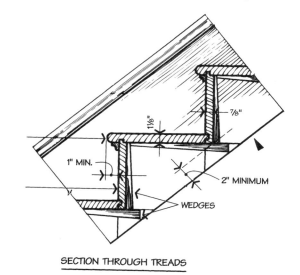

SECTION THROUGH TREADS

The routed closed stringer is usually ⁵/₄-inch stock and is laid out the same way the carriage is laid out: by determining the number of risers and the length of tread and riser.

When the layout is made, leave at least a 2-inch clearance from the bottom of the stringer to the bottom junction where tread and riser meet. There should also be about 4 inches from the tread nosing to the top of the stringer. The total width of the stringer will be about 11¼ inches plus or minus.

Set up the framing square again, but this time allow for the 2-inch offset.

Hit the marks with the framing square.

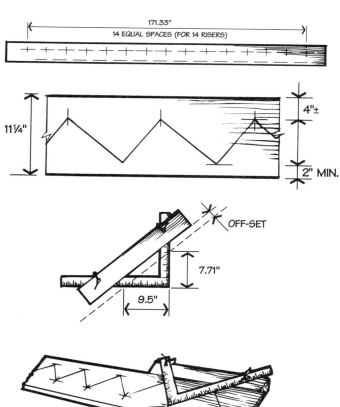

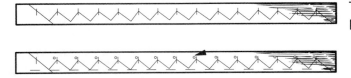

The riser and tread layout will look like this.

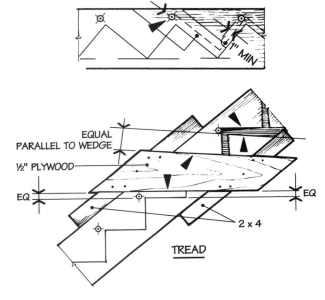

TREAD

Locate and drill 1⅛-inch nosing holes for 1⅛-inch treads so that there will be a minimum 1-inch nosing overhang past the face of the riser. This plywood guide will work with a knife or router. One edge of the guide is for the top of the tread, and the other is for the bottom of the wedge. Clamp in place and do your stuff.

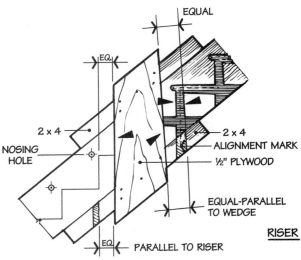

RISER

This guide is for the risers. Clamp in place for either router or knife.

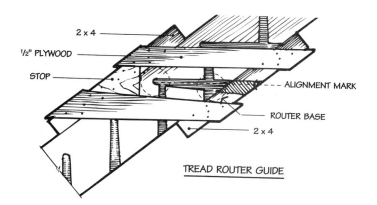

2 x 4
½" PLYWOOD
STOP
ALIGNMENT MARK
ROUTER BASE
2 x 4

TREAD ROUTER GUIDE

I am able to rout top and bottom of the tread with this guide. It's one operation for each tread. I put in a stop to prevent messing up the nosing.

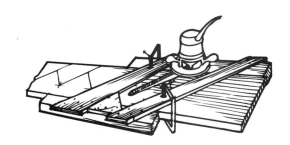

I put the router, with a 1⅛-inch bit, into the nosing hole to line up the guide.

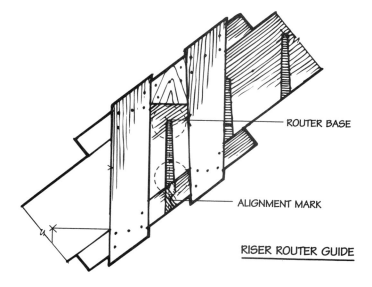

ROUTER BASE

ALIGNMENT MARK

RISER ROUTER GUIDE

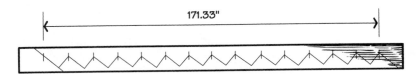

171.33"

The mitered open stringer is laid out the same way to start.

The face of the riser is located, in this case, $7/8$ inch from the riser layout line. This is the outside corner of the miter cut.

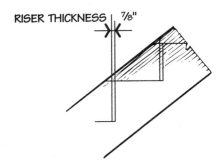

RISER THICKNESS $7/8$"

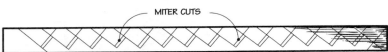

MITER CUTS

The stringer is all laid out and ready to be cut with a power saw and guide or a handsaw. I prefer the handsaw.

The finished routed closed stringer.

The finished mitered open stringer.

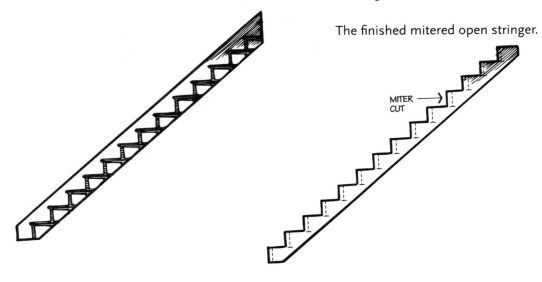

MITER CUT

Risers and treads stocked at lumber yards are either shiplapped and grooved . . .

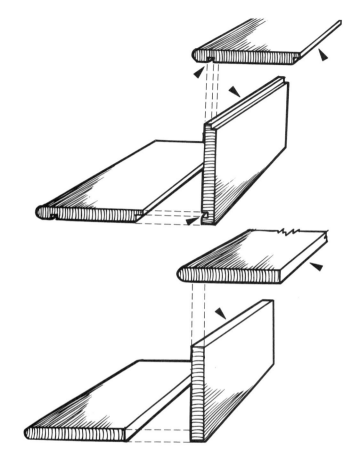

. . . or square edged. Both tread styles are round nosed. This square-edged style must be scribed and fitted for good joints.

At the joint where riser and tread interlock (front and back), wedges and blocks are glued as you progress. The wedges are driven in to force the face of the tread and riser against the face of the routed stringer. Don't spare the glue.

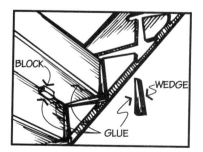

BLOCK

WEDGE

GLUE

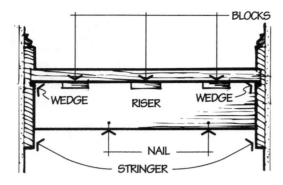

The routed closed-stringer stairway does not have carriages because it is assembled from the underside. Start at the top, installing the tread first.

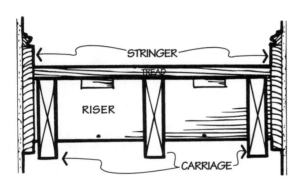

The scribed-and-butted closed stringer does have carriages, and it is assembled from the topside, starting from the top and putting in the tread first.

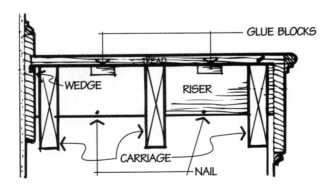

The combination open-and-closed stringer uses carriages and is assembled from the topside, starting from the bottom and putting in the risers first.

Hardwood Flooring

Nailing hardwood flooring is greatly eased with the use of the nailing machine. These machines can be rented.

The old flooring hammer will also do the trick. This hammer weighs about 25 ounces and has a little bigger head and a longer handle. The head is also a harder steel than a standard hammer to handle the hard flooring nails.

No matter what tool you use, the bent-over position is the one assumed for the whole job.

It's best to have the flooring stock on the job a few days in the heated house, preferably unbundled, so that the strips can adjust to the climate.

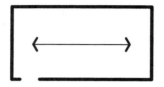

The strips are best laid running the long way in the room.

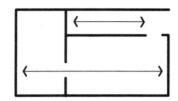

When a room opens to another room or hall, keep the strips running in the same direction.

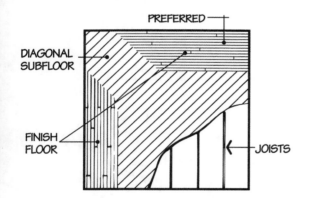

The strips can go either way with diagonal subflooring, but the strongest condition is to run the strips perpendicular to the joists. With diagonal subflooring, this is always possible.

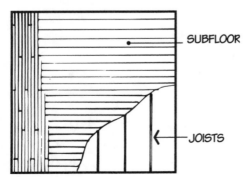

With the subfloor running perpendicular to the joists, the finished floor should run perpendicular to the subfloor for the strongest condition.

With plywood subflooring, the strongest condition is with the strips running perpendicular to the joists, but either way is OK.

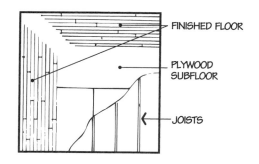

FINISHED FLOOR

PLYWOOD SUBFLOOR

JOISTS

The first thing to do before starting the flooring is a clean sweep.

Then roll out 15# building paper on the floor being laid. Lap the edges a few inches to keep dust, dirt, and dampness from the flooring.

To establish the location of the first strip of flooring, snap a chalk line or stretch a string 6 or 8 inches from the wall and parallel. The string is better because the paper is liable to move, changing the chalk-line location. Start the first strip ½ inch from the wall and keep it parallel to the string or chalk line.

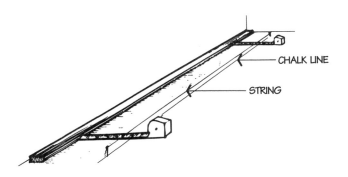

CHALK LINE

STRING

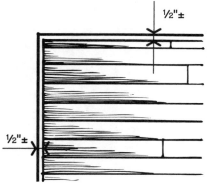

½"±

½"±

PLAN

The flooring is kept about ½ inch away from the wall all around to allow the flooring to expand.

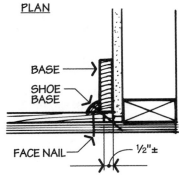

BASE

SHOE BASE

FACE NAIL

½"±

The base or shoe base covers this space.

6" TO 8"

Face-nail this first piece using a cutoff finish nail to predrill. Lay out a few rows ahead so you just have to move the strips into place and nail them home. Stagger the joints 6 to 8 inches.

The skill required with the hammer is not necessary with the nailing machine.

This is the basic working position for hammer and machine.

The nailing is done between the feet.

Drive the nail almost home, just short of hitting the flooring with the hammer.

Lay a round nail set on the head and drive it home with the hammer, being careful not to hit the flooring.

The machine, loaded with nails, is placed over the edge of the flooring and pounded with a heavy mallet. It's the way to go.

Mix short pieces with long ones; but in halls and doorways where there is a lot of traffic, use long pieces. Use extra short and bad-looking pieces in closets.

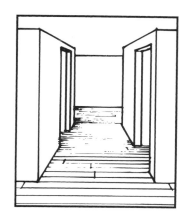

Stand on both the strip going in and the previous one to align and to hold it in place.

Use a block of flooring material to take the hammer blows if a piece of flooring is tough to get in tightly. The nailing machine acts the same way when it's pounded with the heavy mallet.

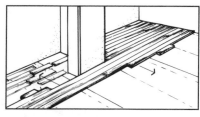

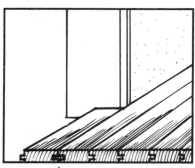

When working from a wall alongside a closet, lay the floor up to the closet face and reverse the flooring going into the closet. When you reverse, the strips will be groove to groove. A spline cut to fit will take care of that. The rest of the flooring goes in one direction, while the closet flooring goes in the other.

The last piece of flooring is ripped, drilled, and wedged into position with a pry bar before nailing. Be sure to protect the wall or baseboard with a block of wood.

CHAPTER THIRTY-EIGHT

Countertops

An old-time cabinet maker told me always to use plywood ledger strips for supporting countertops because they won't shrink.

Solid stock will shrink, causing a gap between the backsplash and the countertop.

All plywood seams should be well blocked underneath.

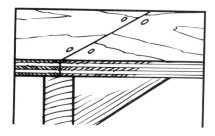

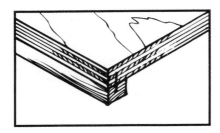

I like this kind of nosing; the top is more solid.

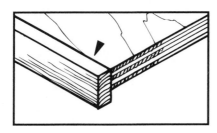

Nosing applied to the face of the countertop can loosen, disturbing a Formica corner.

Fill all seams and depressions; set and fill all nail holes; finally, sand the whole business.

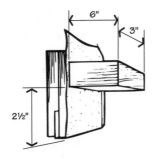

Make up a simple jig from scrap wood to sand the edges.

I have put in many plastic-laminate countertops using a saw, chisel, block plane, and a file, but I now have a few simple tools to make the job easier. The quality doesn't change with these tools, but the speed does.

The simplest tool for cutting plastic laminate is a knife with a carbide tip.

Put a straightedge on the plastic-laminate sheet and score with the knife. It might take a few strokes. Then snap along the scored line. Put the straightedge on the good side of the line. If the knife runs off the line, the good piece won't be ruined. You can even cut holes for switches and sinks with this tool. It has to be used with care because it doesn't control too easily (it is difficult to start and stop the cuts). A few practice cuts will help your confidence.

Another great tool is this pair of shears. After plastic laminate is installed, these shears will cut right to the edge with a clean cut. The sheet should have no more than a ½-inch overhang. This tool also cuts right up to the wall, unlike a router, which leaves a few inches to chisel. The knife cuts the sheets to the approximate size, and then the shears trim them to the exact size after they are cemented in place. A file is used to ease the sharp corner. Someone permanently borrowed my shears, and I have not been able to find a replacement. There are hand-held shears that look and cut like tin snips.

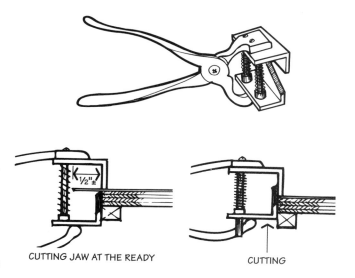

CUTTING JAW AT THE READY

CUTTING

The edging is put on before the top. 1½-inch edging pieces are available, or they can be cut with a knife or on the table saw using a plywood-cutting blade.

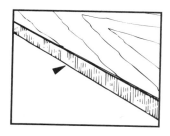

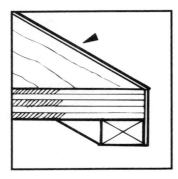

It can easily be put on flush with the top. Put a good edge up for a tight corner.

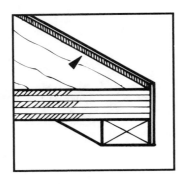

It can be put on with a little overhang and trimmed with a router or my special shears, which I no longer have.

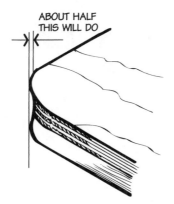

ABOUT HALF THIS WILL DO

Rounded corners are easy if a little care is taken when cutting the plywood top. I like to concave the face a little to be sure the top and bottom of the Formica edging have good contact. When this edging is bent, the face will be slightly concave.

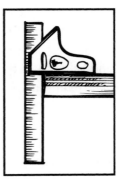

The edge must also be square with the top.

This jig will help.

Plastic laminate will follow large curves with no trouble, but small curves need help. Heat is the help needed, and a hot plate or stove will do the job. First, test a sample piece of edging by resting it a few inches from the heat and timing how long it takes to "pop." Now take a good piece, heat it just short of that time . . .

and bend it around the curve. There should be no cement on the edging or the counter face. You are just preforming the edging. Remember, too, that some contact cement is flammable, so be careful. The preformed edge can then be cemented in place. Another way is to thin the strip on the back side, where the curve is to be, with a block plane. This system has limitations.

A file laid flat on the countertop and run along the edge will take care of any high spots the edging might have.

The easiest and quickest way to apply contact cement is with a paint roller.

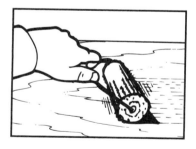

The fumes will make you light-headed in a hurry, so ventilate the area or wear a protective fume respirator.

On a long counter, and when more than one piece of plastic laminate is to be put down, ¼-inch strips of wood about 12 inches apart will keep the cement-coated sheets off the cement-coated plywood so that they can be positioned. Venetian-blind strips, the curved aluminum kind, work even better. They slide out easier.

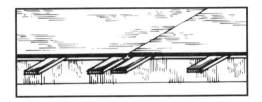

Put a strip on each side of the seam.

Pull the strips at the seam first, making sure the seam is perfect. Then pull the strips farthest away and work toward the seam. This will drive the two sheets together, making a tight fit at the seam.

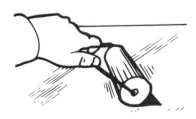

The safest way to cement an odd-shaped backsplash that tucks up under cabinets is with wallboard mastic. It allows you to move the sheet around on the wall. Contact cement is good if there are enough hands to hold the sheet off the wall while it is being positioned.

Once the sheets are cemented in place, they should be rolled with a 6-inch hard-rubber roller to get the air out and make a good bond.

A block of wood and a hammer work, too.
Be sure to go over the whole surface.

Countertops go on before the backsplash, and, like closet shelves, the edges that run along the walls have to be scribed. It doesn't have to be a super fit because the backsplash will cover any imperfections. The backsplash does have to be a good scribe fit.

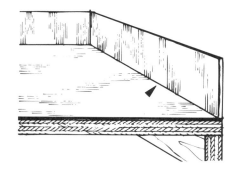

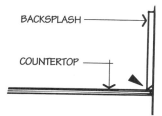

A good tool for this is a sharp block plane. Like any good butt joint, plane it so that the face edge is strong. As long as the plane is sharp, it works similar to planing wood; but when it dulls (and it dulls quickly), the work gets difficult. The procedure to follow: scribe, plane, fit (almost), scribe, plane, fit (you hope).

To plane plastic laminate, hold the sheet, with just a little overhang, at the edge of the counter. Hold the sheet down with one hand while making clean, sure strokes with the plane. Try longish strokes rather than short choppy ones. Keep the plane sharp.

When butting pieces, use the same back-cutting technique to ensure a tight fit on top.

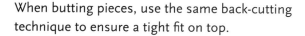

CHAPTER THIRTY-NINE

Cabinets

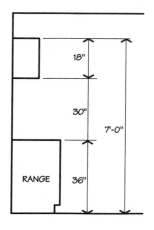

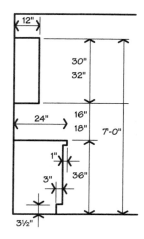

If kitchen cabinets are to be home-made (custom), any size will do; but there are some basic, standard dimensions.

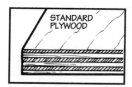

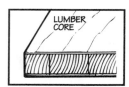

Another consideration is the material. Again, anything will do, but the best choice in plywood is lumber core. It's expensive, so use only where necessary. It's made up of three layers: a veneer on each side of solid strips of wood.

The edges can be covered with solid strips, or a triangular piece can be glued in.

Use the rabbet joint whenever possible. It's strong and neat.

Doweled joints can't be beat.

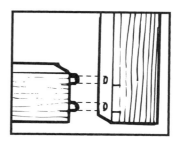

These are minimum lengths. Use longer screws when work permits and predrill. Glue joints where possible. Drywall or drywall-type screws are best, and the best tool for driving them in is a cordless driver-drill.

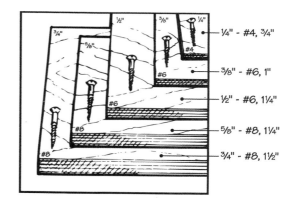

1/4" - #4, 3/4"

3/8" - #6, 1"

1/2" - #6, 1 1/4"

5/8" - #8, 1 1/4"

3/4" - #8, 1 1/2"

Predrill if nailing is close to the edge.

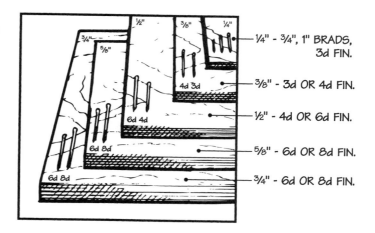

1/4" - 3/4", 1" BRADS, 3d FIN.

3/8" - 3d OR 4d FIN.

1/2" - 4d OR 6d FIN.

5/8" - 6d OR 8d FIN.

3/4" - 6d OR 8d FIN.

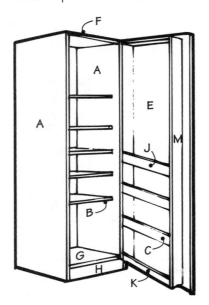

Before starting construction on cabinets, there should be a drawing of some sort that all the parts can be letter coded on.

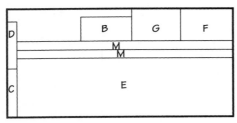

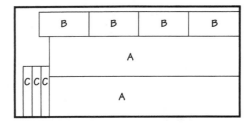

Then, on graph paper, lay out a 4 × 8 plywood shape (about 1 inch equals 12 inches) and fit the parts in. Keep the grain direction and saw-cut width in mind. The number of sheets required for the job is easy to figure from these layouts. They don't have to be fancy.

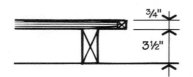

The depth of the base is controlled by the cabinet front frame.

. . . Ths condition is hard to clean.

This is fairly common.

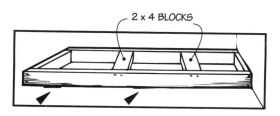

There are many ways to build cabinets, and I like to build base cabinets on a leveled 1½- × 4¾-inch base. Level up with wood-shingle tips. The base is designed so that the interior partitions can be centered on 2 × 4 blocks built into the base.

Pencil the cabinet outline on the wall. Screw the ³/₄-inch plywood counter support ³/₄ inch down from the level countertop line. Be sure to find the studs with the screws. Now it's ready to build on.

Whether the cabinets are cut and fit as you go or precut, this system works nicely. I start with the wall piece that is notched to fit snugly under the wall rail piece (counter support). Keep this piece ³/₄ inch from the wall marks. The floor piece follows. If the base is level, all should go well.

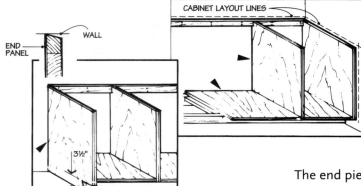

Plumb the partitions as you go.

The end piece is longer on the front to cover the bottom of the front frame.

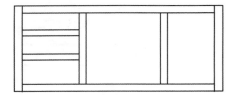

The frame can be prebuilt or cut and fit. If prebuilt, dowel and glue joints. If cut and fit, glue and nail joints.

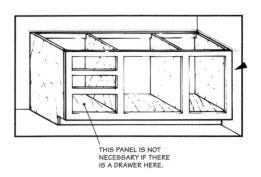

THIS PANEL IS NOT NECESSARY IF THERE IS A DRAWER HERE.

To allow for scribing, make the frame a tad wider and bevel the edge that hits the wall.

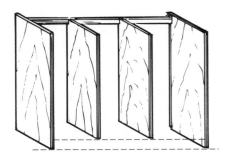

I build the upper cabinets with interior partitions like the base cabinets. Note that the middle partitions are shorter so that they can sit on top of the bottom piece.

The top and bottom are one-piece sections.

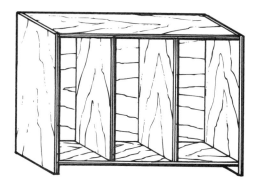

There are cleats at the top and bottom for fastening the cabinet to the wall.

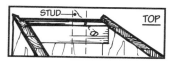

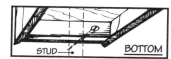

If the cabinet starts at a wall, make the side rail wide and beveled to allow for scribing.

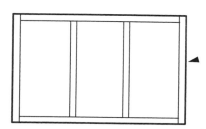

Here again, the front frame can be prebuilt or cut and fit as you go.

The side panels are rabbeted and beveled for scribing.

Doors can be square-edged or lipped.

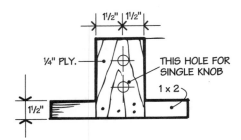

A jig for locating door-pull holes will speed things up.

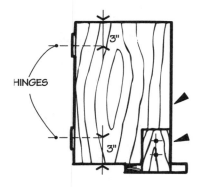

Make it so that when held tight to the bottom or top and flush to the door edge, the holes will be right. It is both a left and a right jig.

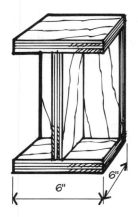

To hang wall cabinets, a couple of wood helpers make the job easy. They should be a little short so that the cabinets can be shimmed to the right height.

When everything is lined up, check the fit at the wall. Scribe and plane if necessary.

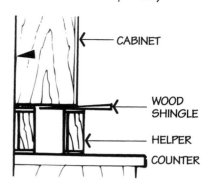

If all is well, find the studs, drill, and screw. It will take a 3-inch screw, so have some soap on hand. Driving in 3-inch deck screws with a driver-drill works best.

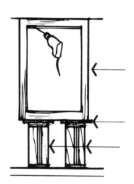

Drawers should be solid and easy to operate. The smoothest operating slides are store-bought, and there are many types. A simple system is to extend a ½-inch plywood bottom to the sides and run it in grooves in the side panels. Use plenty of paraffin or silicone to help the action.

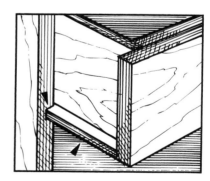

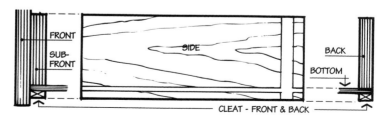

ELEVATION

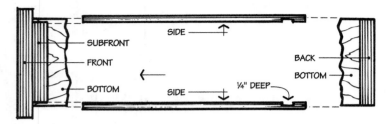

PLAN

Have the drawer guides on hand so that the proper clearances can be built in.

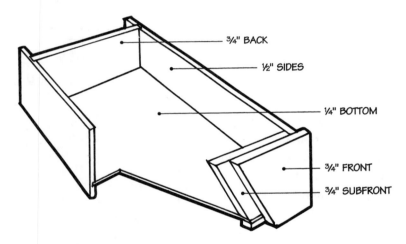

The cabinets will go together better if all the pieces of the same dimension are cut with the same saw setting. In this case, the subbase and back are the same height; the bottom and back are the same width.

Bookcases

A wide wood panel is almost impossible to keep from cupping on the sap side.

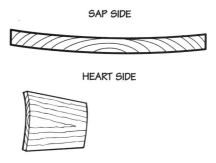

My dad overcame this by screwing curved cleats to the backside of the panel. They pull the panel to a curve opposite the original cup.

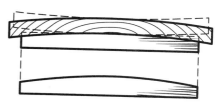

The board will try to cup again but will go just so far. How much to curve the cleats is pretty much guesswork. A piece of angle iron screwed to the back will also work.

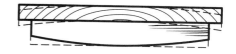

Nothing disturbs a room more than a sagging bookshelf. Stock 3/4 inch thick should be no longer than 30 inches.

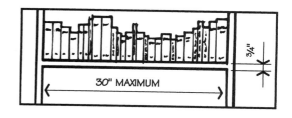

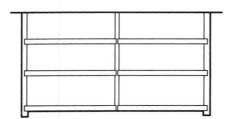

The longer the shelf, the thicker it should be unless it has support front and back.

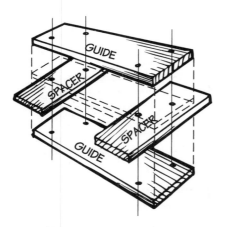

Strong, neat shelves can be made with grooved side panels.

Lining up the adjacent groove is always a tough job.

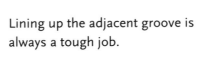

This jig made of ³/₄-inch plywood makes easy work of it. Make the spacers thinner than the board being grooved or shim the board with a piece of cardboard to insure a good grip by the jig.

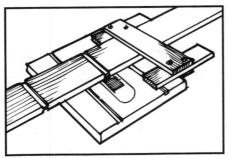

Use the edge of the table to run the guide against. Flip the whole business over and cut the matching groove. Make sure the jig is cutting square.

CHAPTER FORTY-ONE

Helpful Hints

I like to set up a work table as soon as possible. Find a long, free space where a 14-foot 2 × 10 plank can be set up. A height of 37 inches suits me.

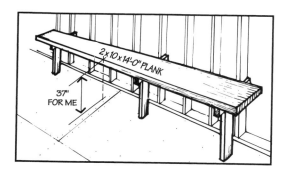

A carpenter's vise at one end is a great help.

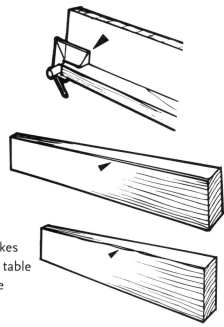

When easing corners with a block plane, run the plane the length of the board in one stroke. This will give a nice, even chamfer.

Short choppy strokes will leave an irregular chamfer.

The same applies for any planing: Long, smooth strokes make for a smooth job. Keep the area along the work table clear so that there is no stopping as you walk with the plane from end to end.

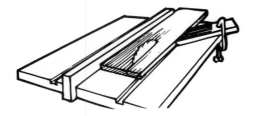

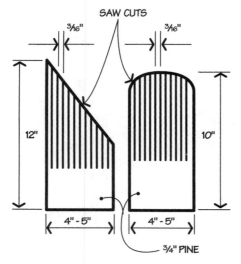

SAW CUTS

3/16" 3/16"

12" 10"

4" - 5" 4" - 5"

3/4" PINE

Spring blocks clamped to the table-saw top keep stock being ripped against the rip fence while you concentrate on pushing the piece through.

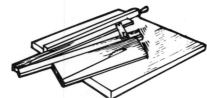

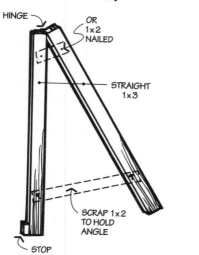

HINGE

OR
1 x 2
NAILED

STRAIGHT
1 x 3

SCRAP 1 x 2
TO HOLD
ANGLE

STOP

A quickie taper jig can be made with two 1 × 3 × 20- or 24-inch pieces of straight stock, with a hinge or 1 × 2 block at one end and a 1 × 2 tacked at the other to hold the angle. Add a stop at the bottom of one leg, and it's ready to go.

This is a handy jig for cutting wide boards and is nice for cabinet work. Spray the rails with silicone for easy sliding.

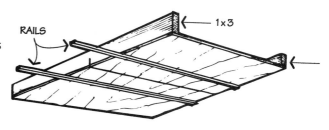

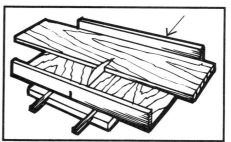

This is a nice jig for making raised panels on the table saw. Spray the rip fence for easy sliding.

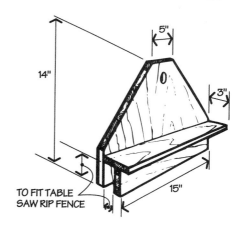

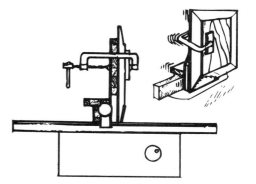

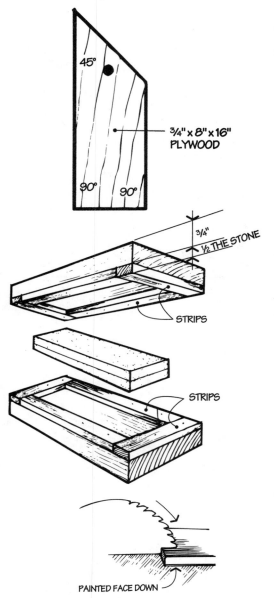

45°

¾" x 8" x 16"
PLYWOOD

90°   90°

¾"
½ THE STONE

STRIPS

STRIPS

The miter gauge on a table saw can be quickly checked if a pattern is kept handy.

Sharpening stones should be kept in a box and wiped clean after every sharpening. A quick way to make a box is to put the stone on a piece of ¾-inch pine (larger than the stone) and nail some strips, one-half the thickness (plus a tad) of the stone on the board, all around the stone. Make two like this and trim to size on the table saw. Keep a little clearance between the strips and the stone.

When cutting wood painted on one side, put the painted side down so the blade won't dull as quickly.

PAINTED FACE DOWN

Gluing pieces of wood together sounds simple, but there are some basic techniques that can help.

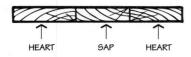

HEART   SAP   HEART

When gluing boards edge to edge for a bench or tabletop, the sap and heart faces should alternate to maintain a flat surface.

They should be planed, slightly, at the center, tapering to no planing at the ends. The edge of the boards will shrink more than the middle, so everything will equalize. If this planing isn't done, the ends will shrink and split. Observe how boards split at the ends.

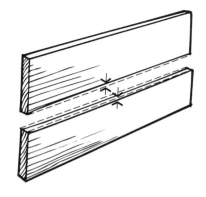

Two boards glued face-to-face should have the sap faces together and the grain running in the same direction, not cross-grained like plywood.

If two boards are cross-grained, the chances for warping are great. Three boards can be cross-grained.

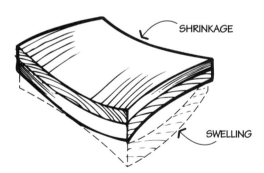

SHRINKAGE

SWELLING

This is the best way to clamp edge-glued boards.

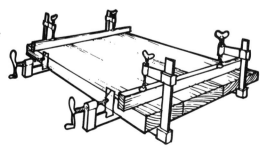

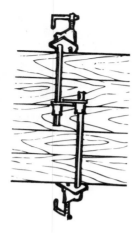

If bar clamps are too short, they can be used in combination.

Here is a quickie way to edge-glue boards. Some weights on the top will keep the boards from buckling.

Miters are tough to clamp, but two blocks tacked on the outside will make clamping possible.

If there is water available, this is a good way to get some pressure for face gluing.

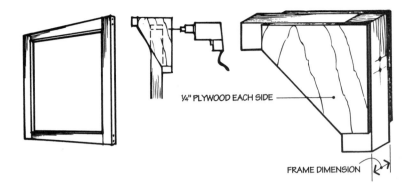

¼" PLYWOOD EACH SIDE

FRAME DIMENSION

Drilling 400 holes in 50 frames (8 holes per frame) required a jig to speed things up. This jig let me drill a pair of holes in each corner with ease.

MARK FOR LOCATING

Twenty-two beams 20 inches thick had to be drilled from each side and the holes had to meet. I made a jig to line up the drilling, and it worked great.

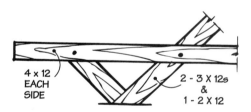

4 x 12 EACH SIDE

2 - 3 X 12s & 1 - 2 X 12

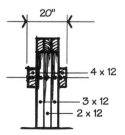

20"

4 x 12

3 x 12

2 x 12

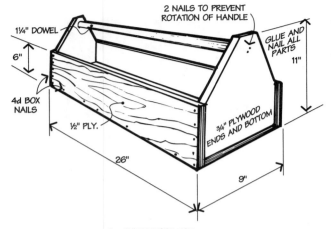

1¼" DOWEL

2 NAILS TO PREVENT ROTATION OF HANDLE

6"

GLUE AND NAIL ALL PARTS

11"

4d BOX NAILS

½" PLY.

¾" PLYWOOD ENDS AND BOTTOM

26"

9"

A tote box to carry an assortment of nails and brads is handy. Size it to fit a mess of tin cans.

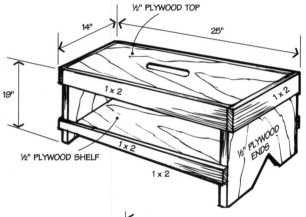

½" PLYWOOD TOP

14"

25"

1 x 2

1 x 2

19"

½" PLYWOOD ENDS

½" PLYWOOD SHELF

1 x 2

1 x 2

For working on casings you can't beat this lightweight "cricket."

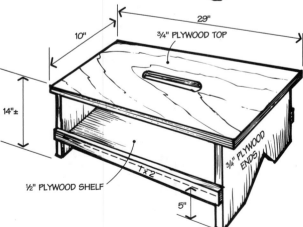

29"

10"

¾" PLYWOOD TOP

14"±

¾" PLYWOOD ENDS

½" PLYWOOD SHELF

1 x 2

5"

This is a simple version of the "cricket."

This electric miter-box bench with swivel top has been a big help. I made it so that the work bed of the miter box is the same height as my table saw. I have great flexibility with the swivel top.

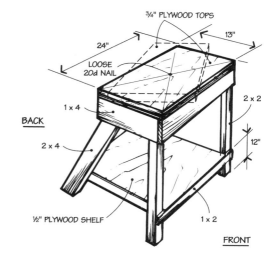

Here's a lightweight table-saw support made of 1 × 1-inch angle iron with plywood shelves.

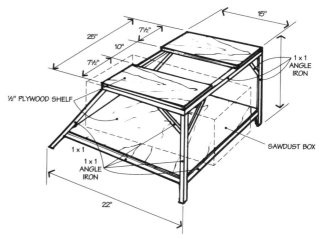

A sawdust box under the table saw keeps the area clean; but when the arbor nut falls into the sawdust, it is almost impossible to find. Keep a magnet handy, and fishing out metal in the sawdust box will be a snap.

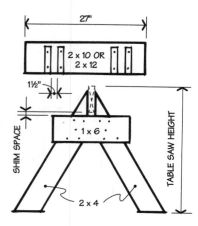

This is a quickie work support for the table saw. It comes apart, is easily stored, and adjusts for height.

I made the height of all my equipment the same so that I could use the pieces with each other.

Getting a Good House

CHAPTER FORTY-TWO

Outside the House

GOOD WORKMANSHIP OUTSIDE THE HOUSE
Where to Look and What to Look For

1. *Mud sills:* Well anchored and level.

2. *Entry steps:* Level front-to-back and side-to-side. Neat masonry work with no cracks or patches.

3. *Garage:* Smooth, crack-free floor (one or two hairline cracks OK), with dropped apron.

4. *Chimney:* Neat, clean masonry work with no cracks or patches. Neat, clean flashing with no caulking at the seams.

5. *Roof:* Good grade of wood shingles, red cedar best. Joints offset on wood-shingle roof. Good grade of asphalt shingles. Straight line along gable ends and valleys.

6. *Venting:* Ridge or gable vents. Eave vents. Well insulated.

7. *Trim:* Well painted. Well nailed. No splits. Good joints. Space between masonry and trim.

8. *Siding:* Well painted or stained. Well nailed. No splits. Good joints.

9. *Gutters:* If wood, good joints well flashed. Well anchored, sloped toward downspouts. Downspout runoff away from foundation.

10. *Doors:* If wood, all six surfaces painted. Weather-stripped jambs. Threshold, if wood, must be well sealed, flat (not cupped) and sloped away from door well. Flashed behind trim and siding.

11. *Grading:* Ground slopes away from foundation, basement window wells, ground-level doors.

CHAPTER FORTY-THREE

Foundations

A well-built house starts with a well-built foundation, and this is the way most of the foundations look under the houses I've built on Cape Cod. I say *most* because soil, topography, and the size of the house are the controlling factors in foundation design. My houses are on flat, sandy soil, which creates few problems. For a small house, I sometimes leave out the steel in the footings to save the customer a few dollars in the budget.

My foundation consists of a steel-reinforced keyed footing that has been poured on undisturbed soil. Steel in the footing strengthens it; keying the footing locks the walls to it, preventing them from shifting under a heavy load, and a foundation on undisturbed soil will not settle.

If the excavator digs one corner a little too deep, it's better to make the concrete in that section of the footing deeper, rather than leveling up the trench with fill. This is a good part of the work to keep an eye on. I've caught some foundation men filling low spots to level the bottom of the footing trenches. I've asked them to stop and shovel out all the soil they've shoveled in, down to unexcavated soil, because I don't want uneven settling of the house somewhere down the line. Of course, it's better to explain what you want before the action begins. Very few people take correction kindly, and letting people know that *you* know what you want can help the job progress more smoothly.

I want my foundation walls to be straight, square at the corners, and plumb, with plenty of anchor bolts to attach the house's sill to. A typical footing should have about sixteen 20-foot pieces of steel (commonly called rebars), which cost about $8.00 apiece, totaling about $130.00. Installing the steel takes about thirty minutes. I also place an anchor bolt every 8 feet around the foundation wall, with an additional two anchor bolts at each corner. At $.50 per bolt, this is no place to skimp.

I remember my early days as a carpenter, carefully setting footing forms with a keyway in place as part of those forms. It was a complicated and time-consuming job, but I don't recall a footing that wasn't keyed on a well-built house. Now, though, I rarely see a keyed footing. A concrete contractor showed me this ten-minute method of forming keyways, although he does keyways these days only when he's asked to. Press a 4-foot-long wooden keyway jig into the concrete footing while it's still soft but not soupy. It's not particularly pretty looking when it's finished, but it's inexpensive and it works.

I've used this angled 2 × 4 method mostly because it's easy to press into semi-hard concrete.

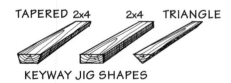

TAPERED 2x4   2x4   TRIANGLE

KEYWAY JIG SHAPES

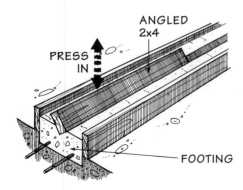

Pressed in unangled, it makes a 1½-inch-wide flat bottom shape. For house construction the keyway doesn't have to be a complicated job or a thing of beauty. For commercial work the tapered 2 × 4 is most commonly used. The triangle is often used when the keyway is cast in place, rather than pressed in after the pour.

No one wants this to happen—not the foundation contractor, not the builder, and certainly not the owner. Saying what you want before the job starts is always the best and easiest way to see that everyone stays happy. I have occasionally failed to spell out what I wanted, assuming it was common practice to do the job the way I'd always done it. That's usually turned out to be a mistake. Cracks like these indicate carelessness on someone's part, and that is not what you're paying for.

I always build the deck, which consists of sill, floor joists, and subfloor, on the foundation before I have the excavator backfill the foundation hole. With the sill anchored to the foundation and the deck nailed in place over the sill, there's very little chance that the foundation wall will be cracked during backfilling.

Delaying the backfilling while the deck is built also gives the concrete a chance to strengthen a little more. You might have your builder consider the procedure, particularly if any foundation walls are more than 30 feet long. It's easier to put the deck on after backfilling, but it's easier to crack the foundation walls that way, too.

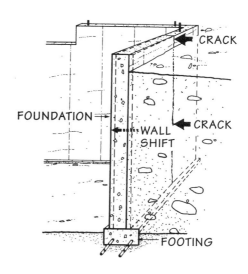

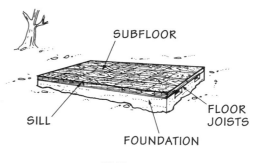

DECK

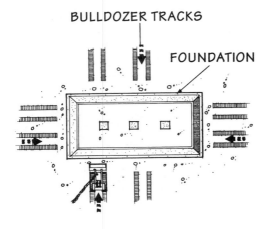

BULLDOZER TRACKS

FOUNDATION

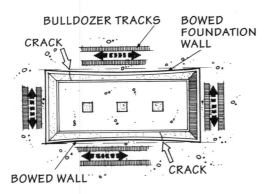

BULLDOZER TRACKS

BOWED FOUNDATION WALL

CRACK

BOWED WALL

CRACK

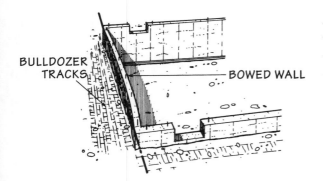

BULLDOZER TRACKS

BOWED WALL

The best excavator I know always backfills a foundation that does not have the deck in place by working perpendicular to the walls, gently pushing the fill into place. On long walls he keeps checking for signs of bowing. When in doubt, he prefers a partial backfill, because he knows he has to come back for a final grading anyway. Getting an excavator to backfill the way you want him to isn't always easy. Often he will "yes" you to death and then do it his way as soon as you leave the job site. I know. It's happened to me. Sometimes I've had a problem as a result, and sometimes I've been lucky.

Running the bulldozer parallel to the foundation walls will bow them in. A bulldozer vibrates the ground it rolls over, compacting the soil below, which in turn exerts a lot of sideways pressure against the foundation wall. My first house had wall cracks, but at the time I had no idea why, because there were no cracks in the footing. I now realize that the foundation was backfilled before the deck was on, that the machine was run parallel to the wall, and that the long wall was a vulnerable 40 feet long.

A foundation I had done for me a while back had this result: I had instructed the bulldozer operator not to run parallel to the walls and to check frequently for any sign of bowing. He did things his way instead. I was lucky; the wall cracked, but it didn't collapse. It's important to keep an eye on things.

All is not lost with a cracked foundation. It can be patched. My first house with its cracked foundation walls was patched with three layers of building paper and asphalt. It hasn't leaked in more than thirty years. There are terrific products available today that let you patch leaky cracks from inside the basement. I have stopped some horrendous leaks using these new products. Nonetheless, it's still best to avoid cracks altogether.

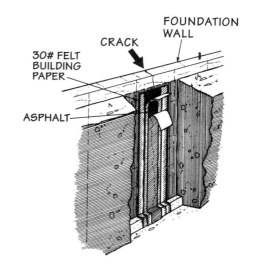

CHAPTER FORTY-FOUR

Leveling Sills

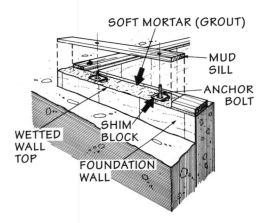

SOFT MORTAR (GROUT)

MUD SILL

ANCHOR BOLT

WETTED WALL TOP

SHIM BLOCK

FOUNDATION WALL

It used to be a common practice in house-building to shim the mud sills level and then fill the space between sill and foundation with mortar. I don't see how you can build a square, level house any other way. These days, though, it's common to see builders simply lay a strip of Sill Seal between sill and foundation. Sill Seal, a 6-inch-wide by ½-inch-thick strip of soft fiberglasslike material, is a pretty good draft stop, but it also sucks in water and does nothing for leveling the sills.

I *have* seen some current builders shim the sills level with wood shingles, but unfortunately, that's as far as they go. Shimming with wood shingles is great for leveling the sills temporarily, but the weight of the house will compress those shingles; and if one corner of the house is shimmed up and another corner's not, you can picture the results. The house won't fall down if the sills aren't leveled and mortared. If they are, though, it's a sign of good work, and you can be pretty sure that the rest of the house will be built well, too. This technique combines shimming and grouting in one step. It's quicker but more difficult than the following technique.

This technique, similar to the standard old-fashioned approach, is a good, quick way to get the mud sills in place, followed by the deck, before packing the grout in. You can come back, shim the sill up against the floor framing, and grout any time. It allows the rest of the job to progress, but grouting this way is a slow process. The steps are as follows:

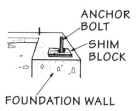

ANCHOR BOLT
SHIM BLOCK
FOUNDATION WALL

1. Install leveling shim blocks at each anchor bolt.

2. Bolt mud sills in place.

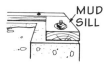

MUD SILL

3. Shim mud sills up against floor framing.

4. Grout anytime by throwing mortar into the space between the mud sill and the top of the foundation wall. Pack it in with the butt (thick) end of a wood shingle.

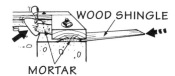

WOOD SHINGLE
MORTAR

On a house I did a few years ago I used both methods, and I was surprised at how long it took my $15.00-an-hour man to pack mortar under the sills. I'm sure the main reason sill grouting isn't done today is this cost of labor. That's why I came up with the faster technique shown on the previous page.

Gluing Subfloors

I mentioned earlier that it's best to put the deck on before backfilling the foundation. Well, if you glue the subfloor in place using a construction adhesive (PL 200 or PL 400), you'll go a long way toward preventing squeaky floors. A bed of adhesive on top of each floor joist, along with the standard nailing, eliminates the movement that produces squeaks. (There's no need to waste adhesive on the perimeter framing members because the exterior walls will hold them in place.)

This is another one of those things you have to ask your builder to do. In a house that's already built, you can check in the basement to see if you can spot adhesive oozing out along the top of the floor joists. Gluing is a relatively new technique, so it doesn't mean bad work if it wasn't done. In fact, I started doing it only about five years ago.

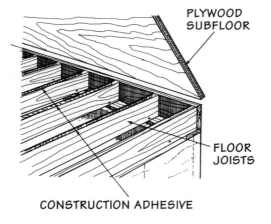

PLYWOOD
SUBFLOOR

FLOOR
JOISTS

CONSTRUCTION ADHESIVE

CHAPTER FORTY-SIX

Masonry Entrance Steps

Masonry steps are extremely heavy and they require a good strong footing on undisturbed soil to prevent sags and cracks. Unfortunately, the soil at the entry area is always soft fill, not suitable for supporting heavy loads such as masonry steps. I've had to repair quite a few entry steps built on slabs that have been poured on this stuff.

A dozen years ago, a mason friend showed me a simple, easy, and inexpensive method that I always use now for supporting masonry steps. A nice feature here is that no concrete shows above grade.

For very heavy loads I use two or more walls of 8-inch concrete block supported by a footing, which should be poured as part of the foundation-wall footing. The concrete blocks are laid up dry, without mortar. The top of the block walls should be well below the finished grade. The top of the reinforced concrete slab supported by the block walls will then be below grade, so that only the finished material—brick or stone—will show

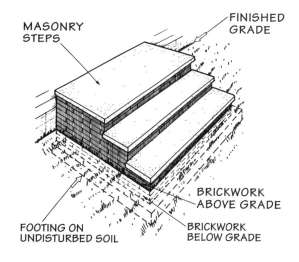

MASONRY STEPS

FINISHED GRADE

FOOTING ON UNDISTURBED SOIL

BRICKWORK ABOVE GRADE

BRICKWORK BELOW GRADE

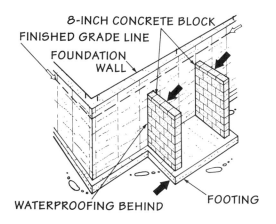

8-INCH CONCRETE BLOCK

FINISHED GRADE LINE

FOUNDATION WALL

WATERPROOFING BEHIND

FOOTING

above grade. For lighter-weight steps I've laid the blocks on undisturbed soil with no concrete footing.

A nice side benefit to this method is that the waterproofing that is brushed onto the outside of the foundation wall becomes an unbroken membrane behind the concrete-block walls because the blocks are laid up after the waterproofing is applied.

The concrete-block walls support a 4-inch concrete slab with ½-inch rebars running each way, with about a 12-inch grid. None of this work is very time consuming or precise. The concrete slab should be level and large enough to accommodate the finished masonry steps. There are other ways to support masonry steps, but this method works well for me. It allows freedom to change the step design. Once again, you will have to show your builder what you want, but if he or she is a good builder, the merits of this method will be obvious.

Supporting the reinforced slab-on-concrete posts is a system to use when no footing or support walls are in place. Compared with scooping out a 7-foot pit, digging four 7-foot holes with a post-hole digger is relatively easy work. I've done this for small masonry steps and when a remodel job called for a new entry.

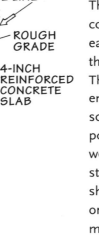

FINISHED GRADE LINE
FOUNDATION WALL
ROUGH GRADE
4-INCH REINFORCED CONCRETE SLAB
1/2-INCH REBARS EACH WAY

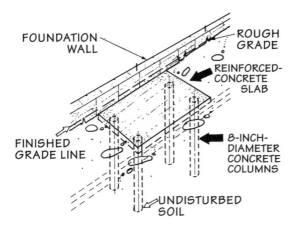

FOUNDATION WALL
ROUGH GRADE
REINFORCED-CONCRETE SLAB
FINISHED GRADE LINE
8-INCH-DIAMETER CONCRETE COLUMNS
UNDISTURBED SOIL

This is another variation, which works best when the finished grade is known. A 2 × 4 keyway in the foundation wall supports the reinforced-concrete slab at the foundation end. Eight-inch concrete columns support the slab at the outer edge. The problem with this system is its lack of flexibility. The keyway must be below grade, so once the keyway is located, the grade can't be lowered below the top of the keyway without exposing the unattractive reinforced slab.

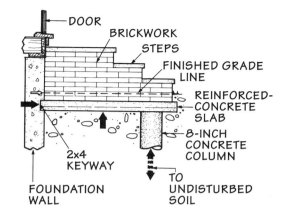

DOOR
BRICKWORK
STEPS
FINISHED GRADE LINE
REINFORCED-CONCRETE SLAB
8-INCH CONCRETE COLUMN
2x4 KEYWAY
FOUNDATION WALL
TO UNDISTURBED SOIL

Garage Floors and Aprons

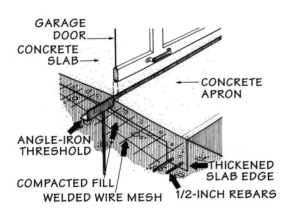

GARAGE DOOR

CONCRETE SLAB

CONCRETE APRON

ANGLE-IRON THRESHOLD

THICKENED SLAB EDGE

COMPACTED FILL

WELDED WIRE MESH

1/2-INCH REBARS

A good garage floor has a smooth, crack-free concrete slab and an apron that is sloped slightly to drain water out and away from the garage. The concrete apron, which is outside the garage, should be 3/4 inch lower than the concrete slab inside the garage. The closed garage door should rest on the lower concrete apron. This keeps wind-driven leaves and water out of the garage.

The way I get a good long-lasting garage floor and apron is to make sure the concrete is poured on *well-compacted* fill. I like sand best. Both the slab and the apron should be reinforced with welded wire mesh embedded in them. I thicken the driveway edge of the apron and put in two steel rebars. I reinforce the garage-floor slab at the dropped apron with a continuous piece of angle iron. These are features you have to ask for specifically because garages are not generally done this way, and there's no way of knowing, other than by the angle iron, if it has been done.

Here is what you often see: a cracked apron, cracked slabs, and water leaks under doors. Thin concrete slabs on soft fill won't hold up under the stress of everyday car traffic. Without a dropped apron, it's difficult to keep water and dirt out of the garage. Even a simple dropped apron with no angle iron will work, but it's easier to get a flat level floor when a length of angle iron is used. Properly set in place, it acts as a form to contain the concrete when it's poured and screeded.

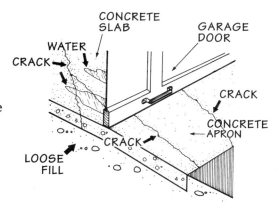

It's neither difficult nor expensive to install an angle-iron strip at the garage-door opening. A few lengths of rebar welded to angle iron (which any welding shop can do) serve to support it in place during the concrete pour. The angle iron is simply located an inch or so behind where the back of the door will be and then driven down with a hand maul to the height desired to make sure it's level. This is a quick, inexpensive, dynamite system for creating a dropped apron and reinforcing the slab at the garage door.

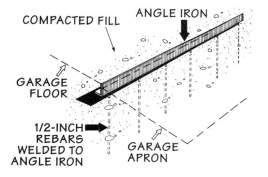

CHAPTER FORTY-EIGHT

Chimneys

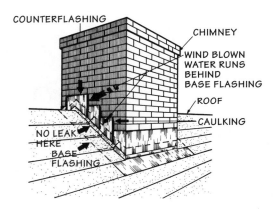

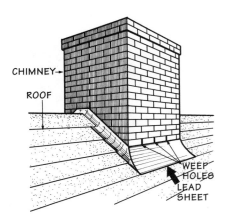

The next time you're driving or walking around your neighborhood, take a look at the chimneys of the older houses and you'll see another all-too-common sight: caulked chimney flashing. The caulking is an effort to stop wind-driven water from getting into the house and staining the ceiling and walls below. Aside from looking bad, the caulking is always only temporary because there is so much expansion and contraction of the different materials that the cracks don't stay closed. You won't see caulking on new chimneys because it takes a few years for things to happen. Not all chimneys have this problem, but I have patched and repatched an awful lot of chimney flashing on Cape Cod, where I live.

This chimney flashing system, called a through lead pan flashing, will not leak. It costs $200 to $300 more than conventional chimney flashing, but you'll never have to worry about leaking. I've seen this flashing system used only on Cape Cod, but it's been used successfully here for more than fifty years. It takes know-how and skill to flash a chimney using this system, and many masons have never heard of it, so you might have difficulty finding a mason to use it.

The chimney is base-flashed (horizontally under the shingle courses, and vertically against the chimney base) normally. This keeps water running down the roof from getting into the house below. My mason convinced me to use the through lead pan flashing system when he told me about the fifty-year-old lead pan–flashed chimney he was asked to check out because it leaked. He spent hours on the roof, running water from a garden hose from every possible direction and checking the flashing for tears. He suddenly realized that the roof had just been reshingled and that the leak was a new one. The light went on! The roofers had improperly replaced a piece of base flashing, and it was diverting water into the house instead of onto the roof. A five-minute fix was all it took, and no more leak. The fifty-year-old through lead pan flashing had not failed after all.

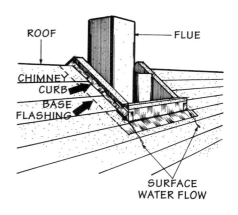

The secret to the success of this flashing is the lead sheeting. Internally, the lead is shaped to divert any water that gets behind the chimney brickwork away from the flues. All the internal water, and there is plenty of it, is diverted out the weep holes and onto the roof. The base flashing is completely covered by the lead sheeting, resulting in a nonleaking chimney flashing system. When the roof must be replaced, the lead sheet that was folded down onto the roof is merely lifted for the removal

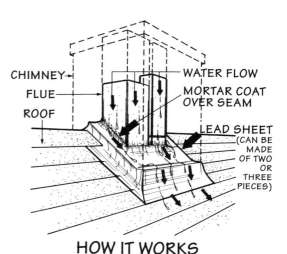

HOW IT WORKS

of the old shingles underneath. The sheet is then patted back down after the new shingles are on the roof.

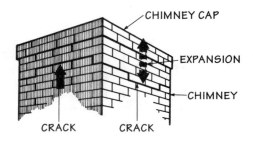

CHIMNEY CAP

EXPANSION

CHIMNEY

CRACK   CRACK

Another common problem is chimney cracks. The top of a chimney usually has a sloped concrete cap cast in place around the chimney flues. When the flues expand from fireplace or furnace heat, they will lift the cap and all attached masonry. The results are cracks at the weakest parts of the masonry chimney. When the chimney comes through the roof, the cracks are usually around its top. When the chimney is on the outside wall, the cracks can be wherever the masonry is weakest. These cracks aren't a structural problem, but they look awful.

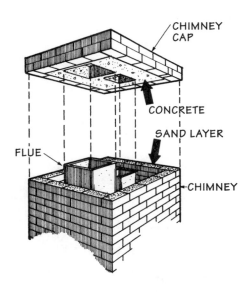

CHIMNEY CAP

CONCRETE

SAND LAYER

FLUE

CHIMNEY

The way to overcome this problem is to force the masonry to crack where you want it to: in other words, to make a control joint, usually by sprinkling sand under a mortar joint. An overhang brick course is a good place for such a control joint. The resulting crack in the shadow will be virtually invisible. Your mason should be able to figure out how to do this if he knows his craft.

CHAPTER FORTY-NINE

Insulation

Insulation is rated by "R" value. It's not important to know what that is, but it is important to know that the R-value per inch of fiberglass insulation ranges from 2.5-R to 3.6-R, depending on its density. If you figure on R-3 per inch, you'll be pretty close.

In a tight house the difference in temperature between floor and ceiling is around three to five degrees. It can be as high as fifteen degrees in a

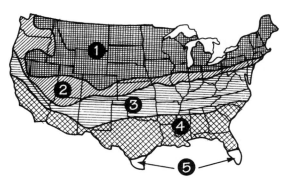

RECOMMENDED INSULATION R-VALUES BY REGION			
Zones	Ceiling R-Value	Wall R-Value	Floor R-Value
1	R-49	R-19	R-25
2	R-38	R-19	R-19
3	R-38	R-19	R-13
4	R-30	R-19	R-11
5	R-19	R-12	R-11

house with uninsulated floors and leaky doors and windows. So to maintain a comfortable temperature in a house, it's important to reduce infiltration and exfiltration.

Infiltration can be reduced by installing good weatherstripped windows and exterior doors. The best exterior door unit I've found is metal. Metal doors are insulated, they're weatherstripped almost like a refrigerator, and they won't warp.

ATTIC ROOM

Exfiltration can be reduced by careful ceiling installation. There should be no gaps in the insulation, and it should be cut to fit snugly around framing members and any pipes leading into the attic. Insist on having it done that way, and then check to make sure it was done right. I've called back a few insulation contractors because of faulty work, and they have always made things right.

Fiberglass isn't the only insulating material available, and some alternatives have specialized applications. Rigid foam panels are used for insulating foundation walls and cathedral ceilings. They are used in conjunction with fiberglass to increase R-values. These panels are more expensive per R-value than fiberglass, and ants love the stuff, so beware! Rockwool and cellulose are used mostly for blown-in applications.

In cold climates, moisture driven from the warm interior of a house through insulation often condenses on cold sheathing surfaces and then drips back onto the insulation, reducing the insulation's effectiveness. In warm humid climates, hot outside air can condense on cooled sheathing or framing members.

A properly placed vapor barrier will prevent *most* of the water vapor from reaching the cool surfaces. It should be placed on the *interior* side of the wall in a heating situation, and on the *outside* of a wall in a cooling situation. Where to put the vapor barrier in a house that is both heated and cooled remains unsolved.

Ventilation is the way to get rid of any water vapor that does get through. The rule of thumb is that attics need 1 square foot of venting for every 150 square feet of ceiling in the rooms below. Attics with a vapor barrier in the ceilings below need 1 square foot of venting for every 300 square feet of ceiling. After a house is built, you usually can't tell if there is a vapor barrier and a ventilating air space or not, but any staining of the wall or sloped ceiling is a sign that air space and vapor barrier are not there.

The natural flow of air is to rise as it heats. Screened vents at the eaves allow air to rise along the air space and exit through a continuous roof vent.

The cathedral ceiling is not as common as the attic room, but the same precautions must be taken to prevent condensation problems from occurring. There must be a free flow of air from the eaves to the ridge vents with no blocked or dead areas. Watch for blocked or dead areas at skylights and chimneys. Your builder must drill holes through the top of the rafters (where they are blocked off by a skylight or chimney) to allow free passage of air from the dead-end rafter space into the next free-rafter space that runs to the ridge.

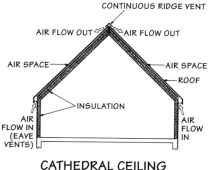

CATHEDRAL CEILING

Without proper venting and vapor barriers, your ceilings will become stained black by the retained condensed water, and both your roof sheathing and rafters will rot. My daughter and son-in-law live in such a house, and while there is no rot yet, the wood ceiling shows the telltale black stains.

Continuous screened eave venting is easy to install and inexpensive. It's available at most lumberyards. These aluminum strips blend into any trim style.

If you see no vents, the house is not properly vented. It's as simple as that. All is not lost, however, because small, round vents, called Midget Louvers, can be easily installed into drilled holes.

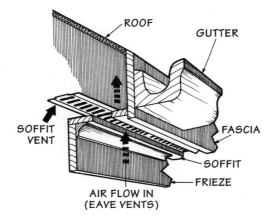

ROOF
GUTTER
SOFFIT VENT
FASCIA
SOFFIT
FRIEZE
AIR FLOW IN (EAVE VENTS)

Rafter venting, most essential in cathedral ceilings, is easily and inexpensively accomplished by using preformed foam units laid in on top of the rafter insulation. They are laid up from eaves to ridge, creating a channel of air about 1 inch deep by the width of the rafter bay. Insulation contractors are very familiar with this product, but you should tell your builder that it's what you want in your cathedral ceiling.

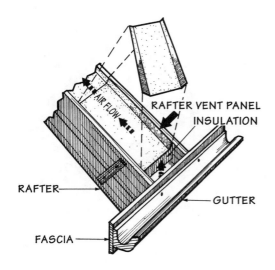

AIR FLOW
RAFTER VENT PANEL
INSULATION
RAFTER
GUTTER
FASCIA

There are plastic and metal ridge vents. They all function the same way: vented air is naturally forced up to the top of the vent, exhausting down and out through the venting holes.

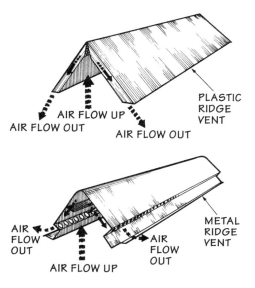

Gable louvers can be wood or metal. They work best when they are as close to the ridge as possible, are at each end of the house, and are the same size at each end of the house.

The thing to insist on here is size, and the rule of thumb is the same as it is if you're using rafter ventilation: 1 square foot of venting for every 150 square feet of ceiling in the rooms below or 1 square foot of venting for every 300 square feet of ceiling if there's a vapor barrier in place. If a screen mesh is used, add 100 percent. Local building codes may call for different sizes, but what I have used has worked well for me.

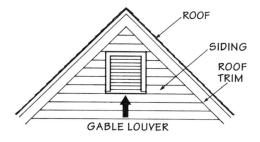

Exterior Trim

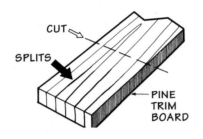

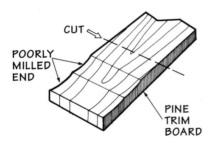

Many trim boards shipped out of the mill are either split or poorly milled. In both cases the bad ends should be cut off. I've seen expensive houses with defective trim boards like these. It is an indication of the builder's attitude. A careful builder will cut off these ends.

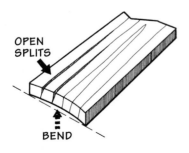

Split ends are often not easy to see, but bending the board will open them up. I always square the end of a trim board. If the end has a split, pieces will fall away as I cut. Splits in trim are to be avoided because they only get worse with age, and they are an invitation to rot, particularly when the splits are near the ground or where water collects, such as at corner boards and window and door trim.

Check to see that all surfaces of exterior trim are painted or stained, including the surfaces that won't be seen. One surface that is often overlooked is the bottom edge of corner boards. Checking the underside with a mirror is helpful when it's difficult to get an eyeball on it. It is most important to paint the bottom-edge end grain because unsealed end grain sucks water in like a sponge, and the end result will be rot.

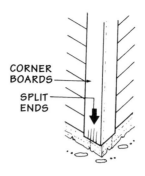

CORNER BOARDS

SPLIT ENDS

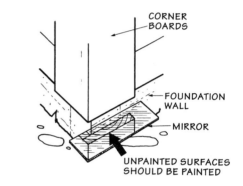

CORNER BOARDS

FOUNDATION WALL

MIRROR

UNPAINTED SURFACES SHOULD BE PAINTED

The back side of flat trim boards must be painted to prevent cupping. Unpainted boards, even when they're not directly exposed to the weather, will absorb moisture, then swell and cup.

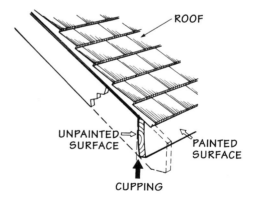

ROOF

UNPAINTED SURFACE

PAINTED SURFACE

CUPPING

Once the trim is in place, you can't tell if the backside has been painted, but if during construction you see that the trim in place is not yet painted, you can be sure that the back hasn't been either. I wouldn't dream of putting up trim that wasn't primed front and back for protection from sun and rain. In fact, when trim gets delivered to my jobs, it's immediately put under cover, and it gets primed fast.

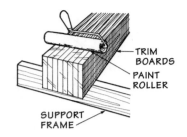

TRIM BOARDS
PAINT ROLLER
SUPPORT FRAME

This is a job you can offer to do for your builder. It's quick and easy, and handling it yourself is a sure way to know that your trim is primed front and back. One coat is enough.

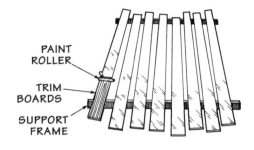

PAINT ROLLER
TRIM BOARDS
SUPPORT FRAME

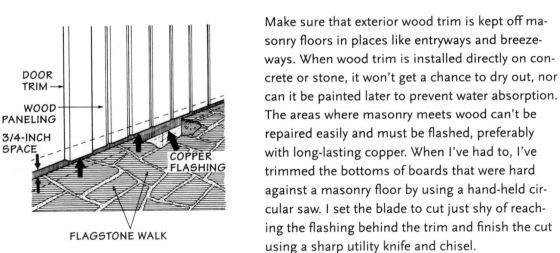

DOOR TRIM
WOOD PANELING
3/4-INCH SPACE
COPPER FLASHING
FLAGSTONE WALK

Make sure that exterior wood trim is kept off masonry floors in places like entryways and breezeways. When wood trim is installed directly on concrete or stone, it won't get a chance to dry out, nor can it be painted later to prevent water absorption. The areas where masonry meets wood can't be repaired easily and must be flashed, preferably with long-lasting copper. When I've had to, I've trimmed the bottoms of boards that were hard against a masonry floor by using a hand-held circular saw. I set the blade to cut just shy of reaching the flashing behind the trim and finish the cut using a sharp utility knife and chisel.

You'll sometimes find an exterior door or gate made up of 1 × 6 or 1 × 8 boards. Be sure they've all been primed before they're put together, or expansion and contraction across their grain will lead to disaster. Even primed and painted, they'll swell and shrink, so the boards should be spaced about 1/16 inch apart. These expansion joints and at least three coats of paint will keep the boards from buckling and the door or gate from jamming in its frame.

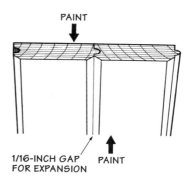

PAINT

1/16-INCH GAP FOR EXPANSION   PAINT

Look to see if nails are set and filled in painted exterior wood trim. Setting nails with a nailset pulls the joints together, and filling, done properly, will make the nailing spots very difficult to find. You'll appreciate this the first time you scrape and repaint your house. It's nasty to scrape trim that has not had the nails set. Scraping over the nail head will remove the galvanized coating and invites rust.

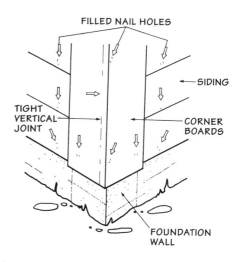

FILLED NAIL HOLES

SIDING

TIGHT VERTICAL JOINT

CORNER BOARDS

FOUNDATION WALL

Unfortunately, you'll often find these conditions. Poorly done nailing, aside from not pulling the joints together, looks bad. In this drawing the nails on the right are not set, and they show up as bumps. The nails on the left side are set, but the holes are poorly filled, forming a depression or crater.

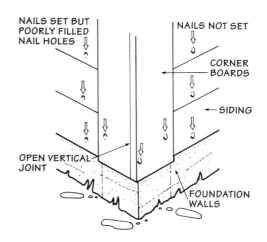

NAILS SET BUT POORLY FILLED NAIL HOLES

NAILS NOT SET

CORNER BOARDS

SIDING

OPEN VERTICAL JOINT

FOUNDATION WALLS

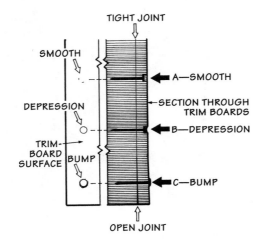

Here's how three nailing conditions look on the surface.

Nail "A" is set and filled properly and is hardly noticeable. The joint is tight.

Nail "B" is set but carelessly filled, forming a depression. The joint is tight.

Nail "C" is not set, and it shows as a bump on the surface. The joint is not tight.

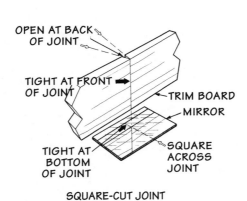

SQUARE-CUT JOINT

Not many builders know how to make tight, long-lasting, square-cut exterior trim joints. It's quick, it's easy, and it will look good for as long as the house stands. The trick is to relieve the back edge of the joint by angling the cut slightly while keeping a true vertical front cut. Where the edge of the joint is visible, such as at the bottom edge of the rake board, the cut must return to square. It's not a difficult or time-consuming cut, and it's easy to trim to length for a tight fit using a block plane.

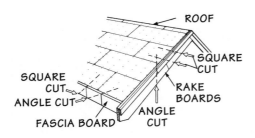

Many builders use an angle-cut joint, thinking it's a better joint. I used to be one of those builders. Here are two reasons not to use such a joint: First, it's difficult to get a good fit. Second, the joint is not stable, and each board can slide back and forth, creating a bump or a depression at the joint.

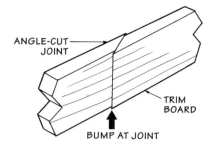

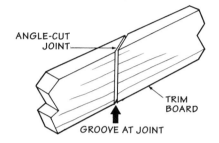

I prefer the quicker, easier, better-looking square-cut joint in most places, but there is a place for angle-cut joints. On vertical trim, they prevent water from getting into the joint, whereas a square-cut joint attracts water.

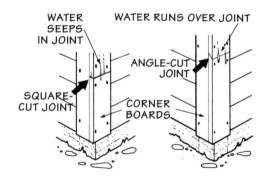

Here's something to look for: trim boards not in the same plane on the surface. You can't rely on trim stock from the lumberyard to be the same thickness from board to board, or even from one end of the same board to the other. A careless carpenter will ignore the difference, and the end result will be an uneven surface.

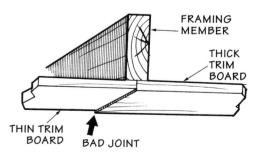

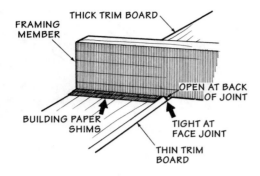

I plane the back side of the higher board when it's thicker than it should be, or shim the thin board if it's too thin. Strips of building paper (tar paper) make good shim stock.

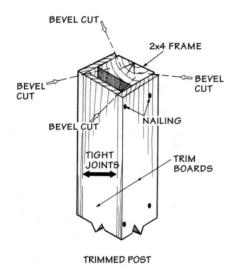

TRIMMED POST

Good joints indicate good craftsmanship, and they are easier to make than bad ones because good joints go together with less effort than bad joints. Relieving the back, unseen edge of a joint is the trick. It can be done quickly by bevel-cutting all the trim stock joints in one session on a table saw.

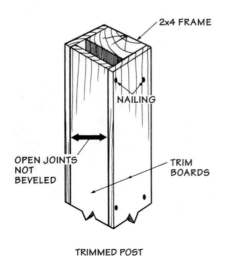

TRIMMED POST

This is what happens when boards are not beveled. The joints are open, and it's a struggle to nail them together. It's a sign of poor craftsmanship.

Blocking for Exterior Nailing

You really need this extra 2 × 4 if you want the siding nails to hold the siding securely in place. Nailing only into the plywood sheathing simply will not do the job. This is another case where you have to tell your builder what you want and why you want it.

Beveled siding must be nailed at each stud, but what happens at doors and windows and corners? In every new house with beveled siding that I have checked out in my neighborhood, these extra 2 × 4s at doors, windows, and corners are missing, and the nails poke through the plywood sheathing. They may be holding for now, but they won't be in a few years.

This is what can happen when there is nothing but plywood sheathing to nail into. Nails will "walk out" as the siding cups. Ringed nails can help here. Splits happen when the nails are driven too close to the end of the board. With blocking in place, the carpenter can nail back from the end of the trim, and splitting can be eliminated.

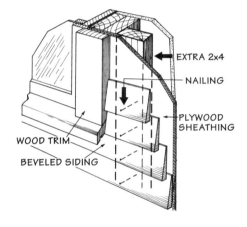

EXTRA 2x4
NAILING
PLYWOOD SHEATHING
WOOD TRIM
BEVELED SIDING

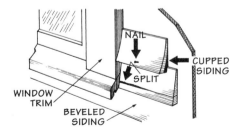

NAIL
CUPPED SIDING
SPLIT
WINDOW TRIM
BEVELED SIDING

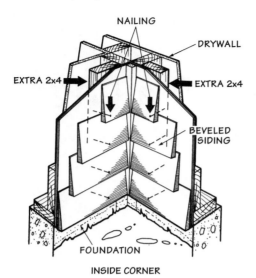

NAILING

DRYWALL

EXTRA 2x4

EXTRA 2x4

BEVELED SIDING

FOUNDATION

INSIDE CORNER

Extra 2 × 4s are required at inside corners, too—not by building codes, but for better building practices. If you want your siding to stay in place, make sure it's nailed securely.

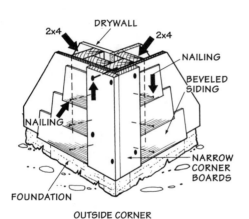

DRYWALL

2x4

2x4

NAILING

BEVELED SIDING

NAILING

NARROW CORNER BOARDS

FOUNDATION

OUTSIDE CORNER

There are many ways to build exterior walls at the corners. The studding at the corner shown here works well for average-width corner boards because there are good nailing surfaces *behind* the plywood sheathing for securing the corner boards and the siding.

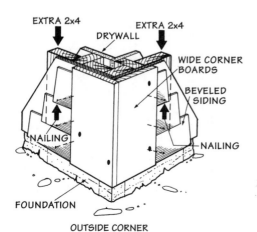

EXTRA 2x4

EXTRA 2x4

DRYWALL

WIDE CORNER BOARDS

BEVELED SIDING

NAILING

NAILING

FOUNDATION

OUTSIDE CORNER

In this case, where wide corner boards are used (strictly a design preference), extra 2 × 4s are necessary.

CHAPTER FIFTY-TWO

Gutters

The function of a gutter is to catch rain or snow-melt that flows off the roof. It carries the water to downspouts, which drain it off onto the ground. Gutters—whether they are made of wood, copper, galvanized steel, vinyl, or aluminum—carry loads (water, ice, snow). Make sure they are fastened securely in place. I nail wood gutters every 32 inches into a framing member. Copper, aluminum, vinyl, and galvanized steel should also be securely fastened every 32 inches.

STRAP HANGER

STRAP IS NAILED TO ROOF UNDER SHINGLES

STRAP

GUTTER

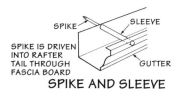

SPIKE AND SLEEVE

SPIKE

SLEEVE

SPIKE IS DRIVEN INTO RAFTER TAIL THROUGH FASCIA BOARD

GUTTER

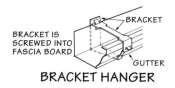

BRACKET HANGER

BRACKET IS SCREWED INTO FASCIA BOARD

BRACKET

GUTTER

Check to see if a gutter is sloped properly by pouring a bucket of water into its high point. The water should run smoothly to the downspouts. There should be no water standing in the gutter.

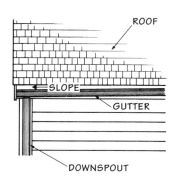

ROOF

SLOPE

GUTTER

DOWNSPOUT

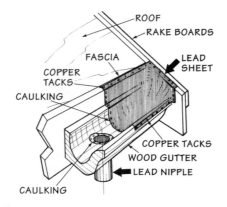

Wood gutters are pretty much regional and I like them; but they are dying out, even on Cape Cod. If you have them or are planning to use wood gutters, make sure they are properly flashed at the ends. That's a prime spot for rot, not only in the gutter but in the surrounding wood as well. Flashing takes a fairly large piece of lead, many copper tacks, and lots of caulking. It's not an easy job, but by patiently tapping the lead to shape it in place (using the butt end of a rubber-handled hammer), I can complete one gutter end in about forty-five minutes.

I like to use a lead nipple at the downspout, and it must be well caulked and tacked. This flashing is an important job, so ask to have it done right and check to make sure it was done right. I've had to repair rotted gutter ends, and it's always the skimpy 3-inch strip of lead flashing that has failed.

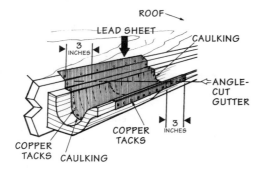

The mid-span gutter joint, which is angle-cut from front to back, is easily covered with a piece of sheet lead. Using a thin strip of lead over the joint might protect the joint for a year or so, but for long-lasting protection it's better to be generous with the lead, caulking, and tacks. This is about a twenty-minute job. Again, ask for it and make sure you get it.

Windows and Exterior Doors

Window and door leaks occur most often between the door or window frame and the jamb studs at the *sill*. The water gets there through the joint where the siding butts against the trim.

Caulking is a temporary fix and looks bad. I have repaired many leaking and damaged thresholds. When the door is on the second floor, the leak shows itself in the ceiling below. Often the leak will show up a few feet away from its source because water will flow along a horizontal framing member for a way before dropping vertically. I fixed such a threshold leak for a puzzled homeowner who had water dripping from the middle of the living room ceiling.

The common errors here are not getting the metal flashing up into a groove in the bottom of the threshold and not running the building-paper splines, at each side of the door, over the metal threshold flashing. Without the splines, water will get behind the threshold flashing and into the room below.

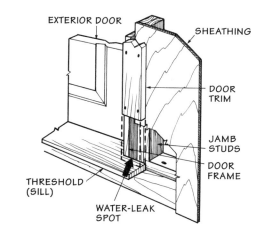

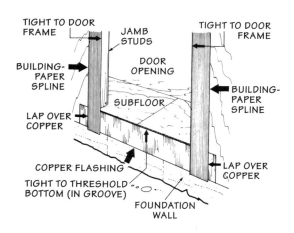

CHAPTER FIFTY-FOUR

Exterior Door Flashing

Make sure your door flashing looks like this.

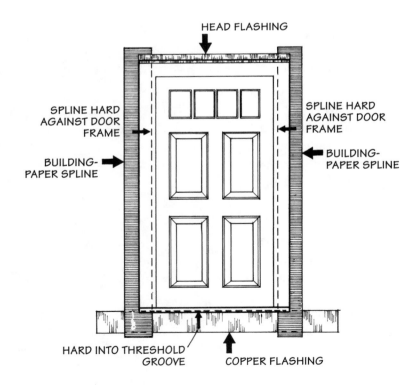

HEAD FLASHING

SPLINE HARD
AGAINST DOOR
FRAME

SPLINE HARD
AGAINST DOOR
FRAME

BUILDING-
PAPER SPLINE

BUILDING-
PAPER SPLINE

HARD INTO THRESHOLD
GROOVE

COPPER FLASHING

Window Flashing

Make sure your window flashing looks like this. In addition to the spline running over the paper sill flashing, the section of spline below the sill should run over the top of a siding course. This will divert water to the surface of the siding.

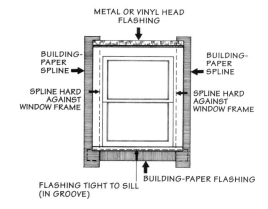

METAL OR VINYL HEAD FLASHING

BUILDING-PAPER SPLINE

BUILDING-PAPER SPLINE

SPLINE HARD AGAINST WINDOW FRAME

SPLINE HARD AGAINST WINDOW FRAME

FLASHING TIGHT TO SILL (IN GROOVE)

BUILDING-PAPER FLASHING

Often, a lot of water enters a house's basement through a window well. Check to see that the ground surface is sloped away from such wells.

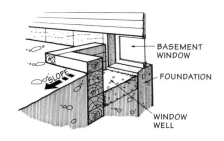

BASEMENT WINDOW

FOUNDATION

SLOPE

WINDOW WELL

A basement sliding door is another spot where water can enter the house. Again, check to see that the grade is sloped away from the door.

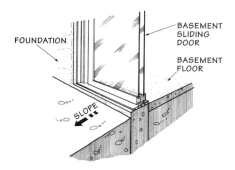

FOUNDATION

BASEMENT SLIDING DOOR

BASEMENT FLOOR

SLOPE

CHAPTER FIFTY-SIX

Roofing

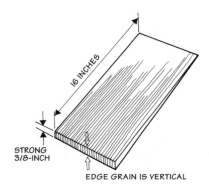

STRONG
3/8-INCH

16 INCHES

EDGE GRAIN IS VERTICAL

I've installed a lot of wood-shingle roofs, and I know it's not smart to skimp on quality material here. Roofing is a labor-intensive job, so use the best—#1 red cedar. The #1 grade is 100 percent clear and edge grain (it won't soak up water like end grain). On 16-inch #1 shingles, the butts (the thick end of the shingle) are a strong $^3/_8$ inch thick (18-inch and 24-inch shingles have thicker butts).

I have seen builders use white cedar shingles on roofs, but the whites lack the natural oils of the red cedars, so their life expectancy is half that of the reds.

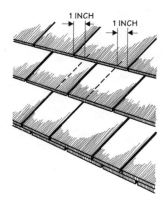

1 INCH

1 INCH

When I do a wood roof, I make sure the joints of every other course of shingles do not line up. I offset them by at least an inch. If they do line up, and if the middle course shingle splits at the same joint line as the shingle above or the shingle below (weeks, months, or years from the time of installation), the resulting crack will be open to the roofing underneath—and a roof leak is born.

The crowning glory of a house is its roof, so it should be the best. The best asphalt roofing is the double-layer textured-look shingle with a 30-year warranty. All the major manufacturers make such a shingle. These textured shingles take more time to install, but they're worth the extra effort.

Check the gable ends. They should be straight as a string from eave to ridge: no lumps or bumps.

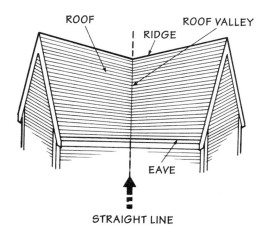

Closed valleys, where shingles touch shingles, should be a straight line from eave to ridge. Open valleys, where a line of flashing separates the shingles of each roof plane, should be of copper.

Shingle Siding

Most of the houses I've built have white cedar siding, and I've found that the best grade of shingle gives you the best-looking and longer-lasting job. I have on occasion tried "bargain" shingles, and I've regretted it every time. You usually get what you pay for, so use #1 clears. They look better, fit together better, and are easier to install with less waste. The butt is almost $3/8$ inch thick.

Look for straight parallel courses.

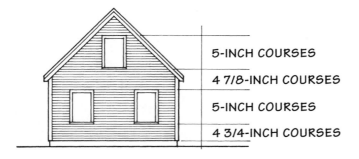

5-INCH COURSES

4 7/8-INCH COURSES

5-INCH COURSES

4 3/4-INCH COURSES

Courses should have equal exposures when possible, but exposure changes of no more than ½ inch are okay when courses have to be adjusted. Good builders have to make adjustments to avoid narrow shingle courses above and below windows.

I run the tops of shingles under the trim at window sills, under frieze boards, and under the rake-board trim at the gable ends. I've found that this prevents the shingles from splitting and falling out.

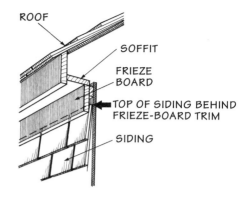

ROOF

SOFFIT

FRIEZE BOARD

TOP OF SIDING BEHIND FRIEZE-BOARD TRIM

SIDING

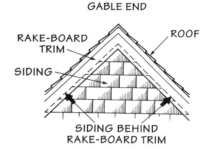

GABLE END

RAKE-BOARD TRIM

ROOF

SIDING

SIDING BEHIND RAKE-BOARD TRIM

Under the windows, this technique requires cutting a groove in the bottom of the sill before installing the windows. Better builders will do this.

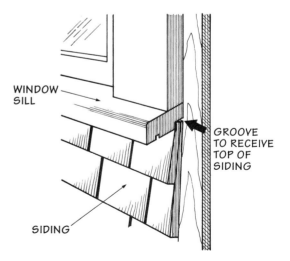

WINDOW SILL

GROOVE TO RECEIVE TOP OF SIDING

SIDING

CHAPTER FIFTY-EIGHT

Clapboard Siding

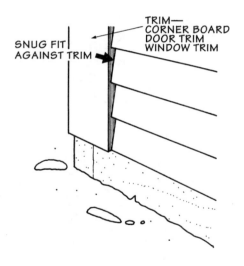

TRIM—
CORNER BOARD
DOOR TRIM
WINDOW TRIM

SNUG FIT
AGAINST TRIM

A good clapboard job starts with good material. The best clapboards are clear, vertical-grain red cedar and redwood.

The careful builder will prime the front and back surfaces of all the clapboards before installing them. I prefer oil-base paint, because it wears well.

A good builder will adjust the courses so that a clapboard course starts at the window sill and the window head.

Check the fits at window and door casings and at corner boards. Each clapboard course should be snug against the trim. It's not difficult to get a good fit, but it does take some extra care. The careless builder will have many gaps, which he will then fill with caulking.

Inside the House

GOOD WORKMANSHIP INSIDE THE HOUSE
Where to Look and What to Look For

1. *Foundation walls:* Smooth, crack-free with snap-tie holes filled.

2. *Structural floors:* Solid feel, indicating proper floor-joist size. Main floor beam (in basement) should be steel or "flush" wood beam.

3. *Wood floors:* Laid up tight, squeak-free, proper joint offset, scraped smooth in corners.

4. *Stairs:* Solid feel with no squeaks. Solid newel post. Good joints where treads and risers meet wall. Smooth, well-anchored handrail with good joints. Balusters set into bottom of handrail.

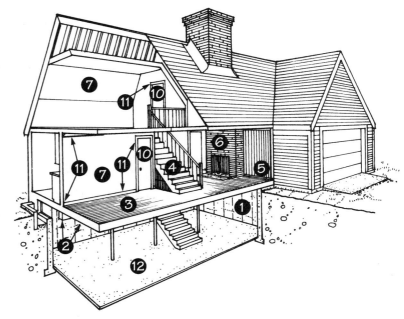

5. *Solid wood paneling:* Good grain and color match. Tongues painted or stained.

6. *Fireplace:* Neat masonry work with no cracks or patches. Clean hearth with no water stains (water stains indicate chimney leaks).

7. *Walls:* Neat drywall joints. No nail pops. No cracks over doors and windows.

8. *Countertops:* Backsplash fitted tight to wall. Neat joints on counter surface.

9. *Cabinets:* European-style hinges and ball-bearing drawer glides are quality hardware. Drawers should operate smoothly with little side-to-side movement.

10. *Doors:* Doors square in opening. Good trim joints at corners. Plumb. Door face touches door stops all around door opening. Doors painted or stained on all six surfaces (top, bottom, two faces, two edges). Even gap all around door jamb and edge of door. Nickel gap for paint (before painting), dime gap for stain (before staining). Smooth to the touch. Good quality hardware, neatly installed.

11. *Painted or stained trim:* Good joints. Well nailed. Nailholes filled. All surfaces smooth to the touch. No repaired splits.

12. *Basement floor:* Dry, no water stains. Minimum floor cracks.

Misc.: Well-anchored towel bars and grab bars. Softened corners on trim, especially on handrails. They should feel smooth to the touch.

Rule of Thumb for Sizing Floor Joists

Floor joists, which you can see in a basement's ceiling, are the wood framing members that support a house's floors. Sometimes builders use floor joists that meet the local building code but that are sized too small to support the floor properly. The result will be the kind of house in which the dishes in the cupboards rattle when you walk across the floor.

There are two quick ways to make sure a house's floor joists are properly sized. The first is to walk on the floor above; it should feel solid with just a *hint* of bounce.

The second way is to apply this rule of thumb:

1. Assume joists are spaced 16 inches on center (most are).

2. Treat measurements in feet as if they were in inches (don't convert—just treat 10 feet, say, as if it were 10 inches).

3. Measure the unsupported span of the joists (usually from the foundation wall to a main beam halfway across the basement).

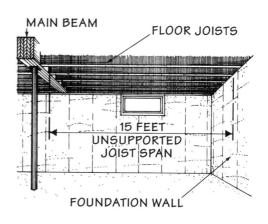

MAIN BEAM · FLOOR JOISTS · 15 FEET UNSUPPORTED JOIST SPAN · FOUNDATION WALL

4. Take ½ of the unsupported joist span (as if it were inches, remember), then add 2 inches.

5. The resulting number gives you the minimum depth for your floor joists.

Example:
Unsupported joist span = 15 feet
½ of 15 = 7½
7½ + 2 = 9½
Converted to inches = 9½ inches

This is the depth you should be looking for in your floor joists. A 2 × 10 actually measures a little less than 9½ inches in depth. So if you use 2 × 10 floor joists, your floor might be soft or bouncy. Larger joists or closer joist spacing will produce a firmer floor.

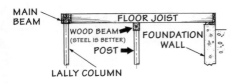

MAIN BEAM — FLOOR JOIST — FOUNDATION WALL
WOOD BEAM (STEEL IS BETTER) — POST
LALLY COLUMN

This is only a general rule for a quick evaluation of existing joists. Factors such as lumber species and lumber grade affect the strength of lumber, which in turn affects the joist-span potential. Fir is stronger than spruce. Joist and plank select structural grade is stronger than joist and plank No. 3 grade.

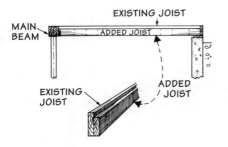

EXISTING JOIST
MAIN BEAM — ADDED JOIST
EXISTING JOIST — ADDED JOIST

A bouncy floor isn't dangerous, but it is annoying when the dishes rattle. I have remedied the situation in some houses by placing a secondary beam under the floor joists, halfway between the foundation wall and the main beam. This new beam doesn't have to be very big, because it's not carrying much of a load. A wood beam works, but it will probably have to be shimmed up snug to the joist bottoms as it shrinks.

Another solution is to stiffen each joist by adding a smaller joist to it on either side, well nailed. This system has the advantage of not requiring posts.

Main Carrying Beam

This is the best and most common system for the main carrying beam, which supports the floor joists at mid-span between the foundation walls.

The steel beam is heavy, but it can be delivered right onto the foundation wall. Some suppliers will even set it in place. When it is delivered onto the wall, it can be shoved over to the beam pockets without too much trouble. I did it alone with my first house. Once it's in place, a 2 × 6 nailing plate is bolted or power-nailed to its top surface.

The joists sit directly on the nailing plate at one end and on the foundation wall's mud sill on the other. Because these two elements are the same size, their shrinkage under the floor joists will be equal. The floor will remain level.

This system takes more time to build, but it's as good as the dropped "I" beam, and it saves headroom because the beam is up within the joist space rather than below it.

DROPPED "I" BEAM

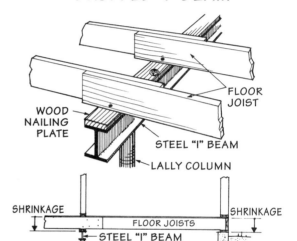

WOOD NAILING PLATE
FLOOR JOIST
STEEL "I" BEAM
LALLY COLUMN

SHRINKAGE
FLOOR JOISTS
STEEL "I" BEAM
SHRINKAGE
LALLY COLUMN
FOUNDATION WALL

FLUSH WOOD BEAM

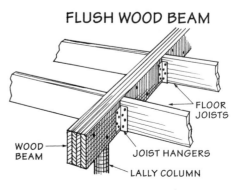

FLOOR JOISTS
WOOD BEAM
JOIST HANGERS
LALLY COLUMN

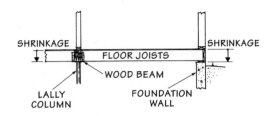

In this system, there will be a little uneven shrinkage as the mud sill ages, but this is a minor factor when the sill is a 2 × 6.

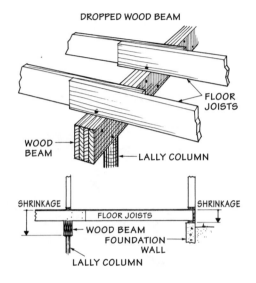

If you see this beam system in your house, expect trouble. This is the worst system, and one I never use.

The shrinkage problem under the floor joists is obvious here. The deeper the wood beam, the more the shrinkage difference. Using unseasoned lumber will make the problem even worse.

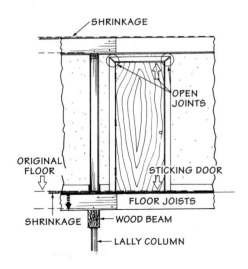

If you see gaps under baseboards, cracked walls (especially at the upper corner of door openings), gaps in trim joints, and doors that stick, go to the basement and you'll most likely find the dropped wood beam.

Fortunately, all is not lost with the dropped wood-beam system. A "telepost" (telescoping post) or any post and jack combination can be used to jack up the beam. Just be sure to set your new posts or jacks close to the existing lally columns so that they'll bear on the column footings under the concrete floor.

The jacking has to be done a little at a time so as not to create new cracks in the walls. This can take weeks, depending on how bad things actually are. I recently inspected a house less than two years old that has a dropped wood beam and all the classic problems that follow. The beam has been in the process of being jacked up for two months, and it's not finished yet.

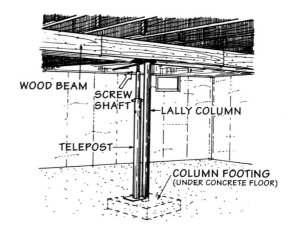

WOOD BEAM

SCREW SHAFT

LALLY COLUMN

TELEPOST

COLUMN FOOTING
(UNDER CONCRETE FLOOR)

Interior Blocking

At the bottom of both sides of door openings, there is a lot of nailing in many directions. The door frame is nailed in one direction, and the drywall, casings, and baseboards are nailed from both sides of the wall. If the door is going to hang properly in its frame, the bottom of each side of the opening has to be aligned accurately and anchored securely to the floor.

Blocks placed on edge between the floor joists on each side of the door opening stabilize this important area. You can check in the basement for this blocking.

Even where there isn't a door opening, there should be solid wood blocking every 24 inches under wall partitions that run parallel to the floor joists. Above, similarly spaced blocking should be laid flat between the ceiling joists. The result is solid nailing and adequate support for interior wall framing.

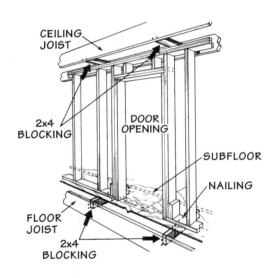

CEILING JOIST

2x4 BLOCKING

DOOR OPENING

SUBFLOOR

NAILING

FLOOR JOIST

2x4 BLOCKING

This is what happens when there is no blocking under partitions that run parallel to the floor joists. The plywood subfloor isn't a good nailing surface, and it will sag under the weight of the partition. I have fixed these sags by jacking the floor up from the basement below and then nailing in the blocking that should have been put there when the house was built.

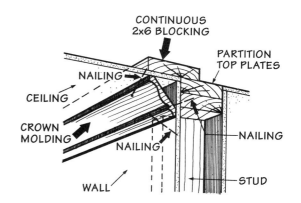

Bad-looking trim work is often caused by inadequate blocking behind it to nail into. Large crown molding requires good nailing to pull it against ceiling and wall. A 2 × 4 or 2 × 6 nailed on the flat to the top partition plate provides nailing anywhere along the edge of the ceiling. The bottom edge of the molding is nailed into the studs.

Crown molding is easiest to install and looks best when mid-span joints are square cut. They can be cut a tad long and snapped in place, creating a pressure-tight joint that will always stay closed.

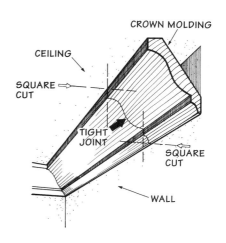

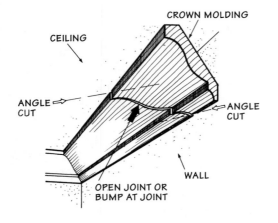

CEILING

CROWN MOLDING

ANGLE CUT

ANGLE CUT

WALL

OPEN JOINT OR BUMP AT JOINT

I've heard builders say (and I used to say) that the proper way to make a mid-span joint in interior trim is to angle-cut it. This doesn't work for two reasons: First, it's difficult to get a good fit with an angle cut. Second, the joint will change with the seasons: It will open up in the winter when the heat's on and bump up in the summer when the air is humid. (It has been said that wood does not shrink or expand along the grain. My experience with angle-cut trim tells me this isn't true.)

The best mid-span joint for trim work is the square-cut joint, cut just a tad long and snapped into place.

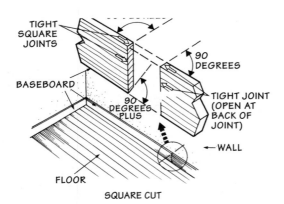

TIGHT SQUARE JOINTS

90 DEGREES

BASEBOARD

90 DEGREES PLUS

TIGHT JOINT (OPEN AT BACK OF JOINT)

WALL

FLOOR

SQUARE CUT

Look for this mid-span joint in baseboards. When the sections are cut a tad long and snapped in place, the joint will stay tight forever. The cut is square down the front and across the top edge but relieved (back-cut) along the back edge so that only the visible front and top joints touch each other.

DOOR OR WINDOW TRIM

WALL

Check the trim nailing by rapping on the trim surface. A well-nailed piece of trim will sound solid. A not-so-well-nailed piece of trim will have a clacking sound, rapping once when your knuckle hits the trim and again when the loose trim hits the wall. Door and window casings are prime spots to check.

When all the partitions are up, the natural next step is to put in all the trim blocking. Don't forget: For trim to be nailed securely, it needs solid wood behind it to nail into. Baseboards, for example, need a 2 × 4 block at the bottom of the door-jamb studs.

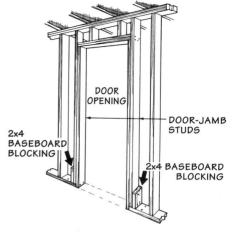

This is how things look behind the wall at a door opening. The door trim usually covers most of the double jamb stud, so the added 2 × 4 block provides the necessary nailing at the end of the baseboard where it meets the door trim. Wider trim requires thicker blocking.

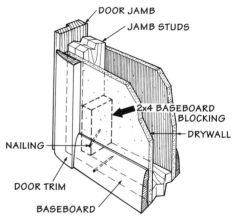

When there is no blocking in the wall at a door opening, you're likely to find a split at the end of the baseboard. The carpenter made a nice fit at both ends of the baseboard, but without solid blocking back a few inches from the ends, it split when he nailed it into place. Rather than replace the baseboard (it would only split again), he patched the split. The patch might be difficult to detect at first, but it will become obvious as time passes.

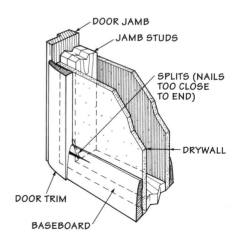

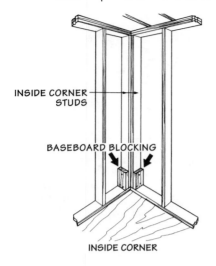

INSIDE CORNER STUDS

BASEBOARD BLOCKING

INSIDE CORNER

Inside corners need blocking, too. It's the same story: 2 × 4 blocks so that there's nailing at the top of the baseboard in the corner and far enough from the end so that the nail won't split the trim. It doesn't take much time to put the baseboard blocks in, and there are always enough scraps of wood around. They don't have to be cut to a specific length, just nailed in place.

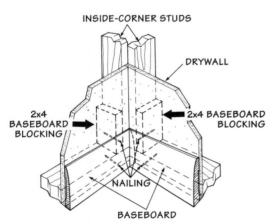

INSIDE-CORNER STUDS

DRYWALL

2x4 BASEBOARD BLOCKING

2x4 BASEBOARD BLOCKING

NAILING

BASEBOARD

This is what an inside corner should look like behind the walls. The inside-corner studs allow only 1 inch of nailing after the ½ inch thickness for the drywall is taken into account. By adding 2 × 4 blocks, the solid nailing extends 2½ inches from the corner in each direction.

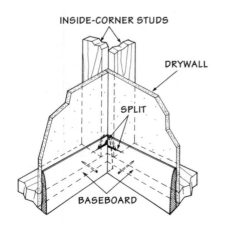

INSIDE-CORNER STUDS

DRYWALL

SPLIT

BASEBOARD

Take a look at the baseboards at inside corners. If there is no blocking behind the walls, you might find these patched splits. To avoid splitting when there's no blocking in place, a careful carpenter will predrill an angled nail hole. Anything that secures the baseboard in place is fine, but splits are *not* acceptable.

A good builder will provide plenty of blocking. A bathroom is a good example of the need for solid nailing surfaces behind the walls. Tub and shower stalls need blocking for nailing along their support flanges at the top and sides. Grab bars have to be well anchored. Even towel bars need light, 3/4-inch blocking. The wider the blocking boards, the more leeway there is for height location.

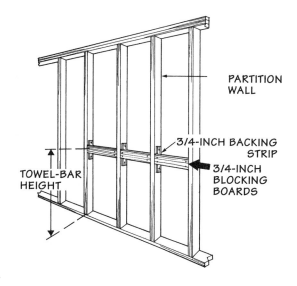

PARTITION WALL

3/4-INCH BACKING STRIP

3/4-INCH BLOCKING BOARDS

TOWEL-BAR HEIGHT

CHAPTER SIXTY-THREE

Stairs

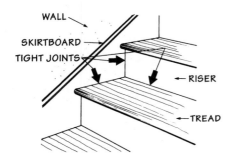

A well-built stairway should not squeak. Walk up and down the right side, left side, and middle of a stairway—you should hear nothing but your footfalls. Check for good tight joints where the risers and treads meet the skirtboard along the wall. Also check for good tight joints where the back of the treads meet the bottoms of the risers.

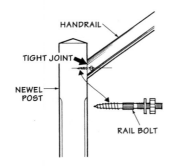

Installing handrails on stairways is a difficult carpentry job. A place to check for good work is the joint where the handrail meets the newel post. You should find a good tight fit, securely fastened together with a rail bolt: a combination lag screw and nut and bolt. Nailing this joint together will not do.

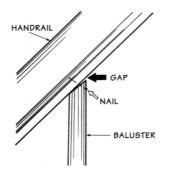

A carpenter's shortcut for installing balusters is to angle-cut the tops and toenail them to the bottom of the handrail. The resulting fit between the baluster and the rail is often bad. Worse, the baluster is sometimes split by the nailing. This is not a good way to install balusters.

The best way to install balusters is to drill holes in the treads and in the bottom of the handrail to receive each baluster. It's a tough job, but a good stairbuilder wouldn't do it any other way.

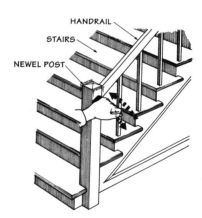

If you have a newel post, test how secure it is by punching the sides of the post with the side of your fist. It should feel and sound solid. A loose newel post only gets worse with use, and it isn't easy to fix one after the house is finished.

Check in the basement to see if the newel post is well anchored. It takes a lot of punishment and must be securely braced in all directions. Solid backing cut from floor joist material works best when it's wedged tightly against the sides of the work and screwed in place.

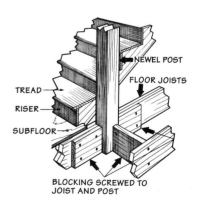

The blocking must be installed so that its ends, not its edges, brace the post. Major shrinkage occurs across the grain, and this, in time, would create a loose joint between blocks and post.

This newel-post anchoring system is just one of many ways that I've seen used, and it has worked well for me.

Paneling

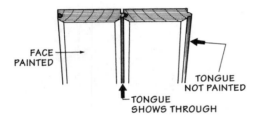

A careful builder will paint or stain the tongues of interior wood paneling before installation. Even though interior tongue-and-groove paneling is nailed tight, the boards will shrink during dry time (usually winter, when the heat is turned on), revealing the tongue. Painting or staining the tongues will camouflage them so that the shrinkage cracks won't be so obvious.

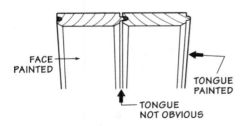

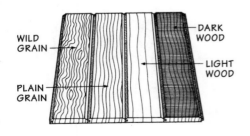

A builder who cares about what he's doing when he installs wood paneling will match tone, color, and grain for the best possible appearance. Wild grain looks bad next to plain grain. One piece of light wood looks out of place on a dark wall, and vice-versa.

Not every builder has this sense. I was checking a job for a builder friend when I noticed that the paneling in the front entry had mostly medium-brown wood except for an oddball dark board here and there. Those boards really jumped out at me. My friend simply didn't understand what I was talking about.

You might want to match the panel boards yourself. A quick way to arrive at a good match is to arrange the boards around the room so you can easily spot the different surfaces. Then it's easy to put the most pleasing matches next to each other. The oddball panels can be cut for trim pieces.

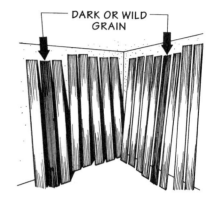

DARK OR WILD GRAIN

Bookshelf Tip

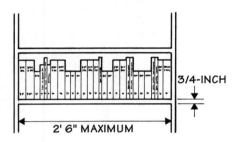

3/4-INCH

2' 6" MAXIMUM

Nothing looks worse than sagging bookshelves. Pine shelves, $3/4$ inch thick, should span no more than 2 feet, 6 inches. Thicker shelves or hardwood shelves can span more, but most bookshelves I have seen are $3/4$-inch pine and usually sag.

CHAPTER SIXTY-SIX

Trim Tip

Square-cut trim as it comes from the lumber yard has hard corners along its edges. These edges dent easily, paint wears off, and they are uncomfortable to the touch. Check door frames, window frames, shelving, and handrails. The careful builder will soften these corners with a sharp block plane or sandpaper. Little details like these provide clues about quality, both seen and unseen, throughout the house.

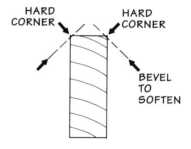

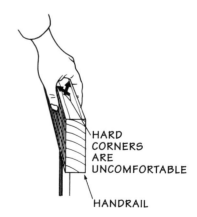

Fireplace Cracks

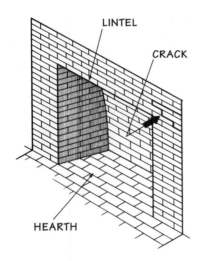

LINTEL

CRACK

HEARTH

It's all too common to find cracks on the fireplace wall. Structurally, this is no problem; the fireplace will not collapse. But it doesn't look too great. Most cracks in the fireplace wall are caused by the fire heating the angle-iron lintel over the opening. The lintel expands and pushes against the masonry, resulting in cracks at the weakest points. These cracks can never be repaired to look as good as new, because the joints are wider, and the old mortar color is almost impossible to match in the new mortar joints.

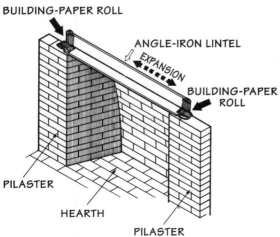

BUILDING-PAPER ROLL

ANGLE-IRON LINTEL

EXPANSION

BUILDING-PAPER ROLL

PILASTER

HEARTH

PILASTER

This is the system my mason uses to prevent fireplace cracks. His trick is keeping the masonry away from the ends of the angle-iron lintel. Rolled up strips of building paper (tar paper) at the ends of the lintel serve as expansion gaskets. The lintel can contract and expand freely. He takes the same precautions at the ends of the metal damper. If you're having your house built, make sure your mason is aware of this tip; but don't be surprised if he doesn't want to hear it.

Bowed Studs

If you're building, check the cabinet walls for bowed studs, using a straight 2 × 4. This used to be standard practice years ago, but I know most builders no longer bother. Holding a long straight 2 × 4 against the studs of an interior partition (exterior partitions are usually straightened by the exterior sheathing) will reveal the bowed stud.

When two studs are bowed in opposite directions, one toward you and the other away, the stud bowed away might not show up until the other is straightened. It's often easier to replace a badly bowed stud than to straighten it, but at this stage of the job, studs often seem to be scarce.

Check the backsplash on countertops to see if the walls have been straightened. It is very difficult to hang cabinets and fit countertops well on walls that are not straight. Counters should always be scribe-fit to the wall. Bowed studs make this already time-consuming job a lot tougher.

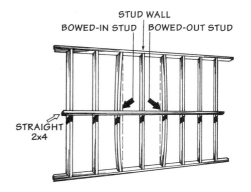

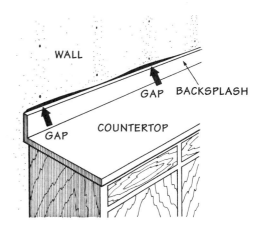

To scribe-fit the counter backsplash, position it against the wall. You'll notice that there are gaps. Set a small compass—the kind you used in school to make circles—to the size of the largest gap. Then run the metal point of the compass against the wall and the pencil of the compass along the top of the backsplash. The resulting wavy pencil line will mimic any ripples in the wall. Trimming the backsplash to this line should result in a perfect fit. (A straight, flat wall needs very little cut off.)

Cabinets hung on a bowed-out stud will be out of plumb unless they too are scribed to hang plumb. On a badly bowed wall, you sometimes can't scribe enough to compensate. It's quicker, and neater in the end, to straighten the bowed studs before the drywall is installed.

It's easy to straighten bowed studs. It requires cutting with a handsaw, a little shimming with wood-shingle tips, then splinting up the stud with wood strips nailed on each side. If you see that this has been done in a house being built for you, you have a careful builder.

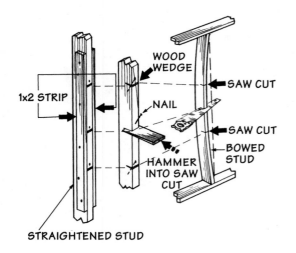

WOOD WEDGE

SAW CUT

1x2 STRIP

NAIL

SAW CUT

BOWED STUD

HAMMER INTO SAW CUT

STRAIGHTENED STUD

Cabinets

Most people can't tell the difference between a well-built cabinet and one that's not so well built. The reason is that these days there's not that much difference in construction or materials. (The exception is the custom-built cabinet.) One detail some manufacturers cut corners with is the hardware. Doors should open and shut smoothly. Look for European-style hinges. They adjust easily, work smoothly and are self-closing. Drawers should open and close smoothly, too, with no side-to-side movement. Look for ball-bearing slides on each side of the drawers. The cheapest slides have nylon rollers.

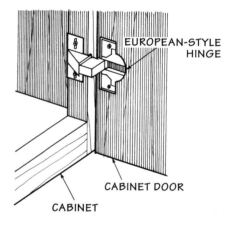

EUROPEAN-STYLE HINGE

CABINET DOOR

CABINET

CHAPTER SEVENTY

Drywall

"Nail popping" occurs when unseasoned lumber is used in drywall construction. Here, kiln-dried framing lumber is a must. If unseasoned framing lumber is used, make sure the framed house is dried out by using heaters. All good builders do this.

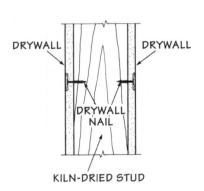

DRYWALL

DRYWALL

DRYWALL NAIL

KILN-DRIED STUD

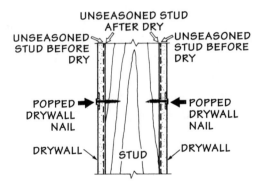

UNSEASONED STUD AFTER DRY

UNSEASONED STUD BEFORE DRY

UNSEASONED STUD BEFORE DRY

POPPED DRYWALL NAIL

POPPED DRYWALL NAIL

DRYWALL

STUD

DRYWALL

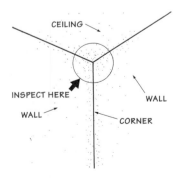

CEILING

INSPECT HERE

WALL

WALL

CORNER

A good drywall job must have neat, crisp corners. The first place to inspect is where the ceiling meets two intersecting walls.

All drywall sheets have two tapered edges and two nontapered edges. It's always preferable to put the tapered edges together for a good, unobtrusive finished seam called, naturally enough, a tapered seam. Unfortunately the nontapered edges have to be butted to each other, too. This results in a butt seam, and achieving a finished look with this seam is much more difficult.

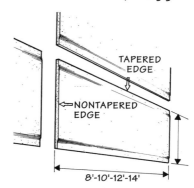

Taping is the key to unobtrusive seams. Make sure tapered seams are filled flush. Make sure butt seams are feathered far enough out so they don't show a bulge when a light is shined along the wall or ceiling.

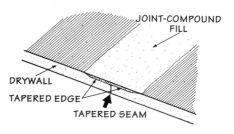

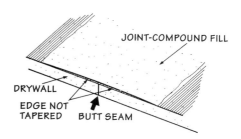

These cracks often occur over window and door openings when drywall is installed in three pieces in these areas. It's more difficult to install a single piece, but I always do it when I hang the drywall myself, and I ask for this when someone else is hanging the drywall. I usually get what I want, so the openings are usually done right.

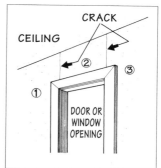

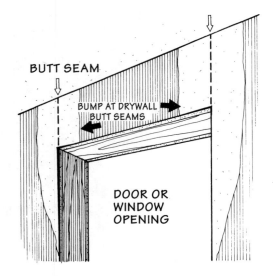

BUTT SEAM

BUMP AT DRYWALL
BUTT SEAMS

DOOR OR
WINDOW
OPENING

Another reason for avoiding the joints at the corners of window and door openings is that the bump created at these joints by even well-feathered taping compound makes it difficult to make good trim joints in these areas. A careful carpenter will compensate for these irregularities and make good trim joints and tight fits against the wall.

Flooring

A good builder will take the following precautions before laying hardwood strip flooring:

First, three weeks before the flooring is delivered, the thermostat is set to 70 degrees or so. This is to dry out the house. And second, the flooring is delivered at least three days before it is to be installed. Each bundle of flooring is opened, allowing the wood to adjust to the moisture in the house.

Butt joints must be staggered a minimum of 3 inches. Nailing (or stapling) should be into every joist, with one nail between joists. So when you look at the underside of the subfloor from the basement, you should see one row of nails or staples between each row of floor joists.

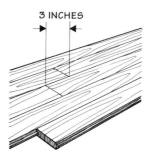

I recently examined a house for faulty construction, and one of the problems was an incorrectly installed oak strip floor. The flooring ran in the direction of the short dimension of the room. It squeaked badly, and there were many cracks between the oak boards. The builder, not knowing how to install flooring, used a nailgun with shingle staples, and once in a while, he stapled into a joist. The subfloor underneath looked like a porcupine.

It's usually best to run strip flooring in the direction of the room's longest dimension. Because wood expands and contracts across the grain (the rule of thumb here is $1/16$-inch expansion and contraction per foot of flooring boards), there will be less movement across the short dimension of the room. A 16-foot by 32-foot room would have a potential expansion of 1 inch across the 16-foot dimension and 2 inches across the 32-foot dimension.

A good floor installer will leave a minimum gap of $\frac{1}{2}$ inch between flooring and wall. I have seen floors buckle and walls shift because no gap was left between the flooring and the wall.

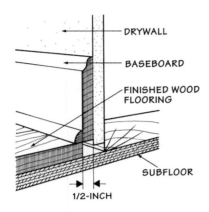

DRYWALL

BASEBOARD

FINISHED WOOD FLOORING

SUBFLOOR

1/2-INCH

If the flooring runs parallel to the floor joists, make sure an additional layer of $5/8$-inch plywood (not particleboard; it doesn't hold nails well) is glued and nailed over the subfloor.

New floors that aren't "prefinished" have to be sanded. I have used many floor-sanding professionals, and it's tough to find a good one. The place to check for good work is in the corners. The good professional will scrape the corners smooth with a razor-sharp paint scraper.

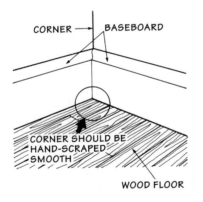

CORNER

BASEBOARD

CORNER SHOULD BE HAND-SCRAPED SMOOTH

WOOD FLOOR

There are two types of floor finishes: surface finishes and penetrating finishes. A surface finish, like urethane or varnish, leaves a tough skin on top of the wood. Penetrating finishes are absorbed by the wood until many coats create a buildup on the surface. The best finish I know of is called a Swedish finish, which combines the qualities of the surface finish and the penetrating finish.

CHAPTER SEVENTY-TWO

Door Tips

Check the tops and bottoms of doors to make sure they are painted. If they're stained instead, make sure they're sealed, too, just like the surface of the doors. Staining raises the grain and actually invites more water into the wood. These days urethane is the standard sealant. Skipping door tops and bottoms is a common shortcut. A mirror will tell the story. Take special care to be sure that any end-grain is carefully sealed.

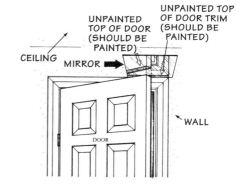

Check the gaps between door and door frame. Proper gaps at the door edges are important to keep the door from sticking. A painted door should have a gap just the thickness of a nickel before painting.

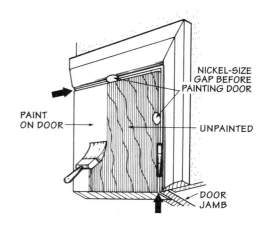

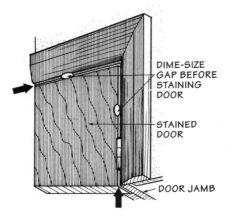

DIME-SIZE GAP BEFORE STAINING DOOR

STAINED DOOR

DOOR JAMB

The proper gap for stained doors is the thickness of a dime before staining and sealing. (Remember, tops and bottoms should also be stained and sealed.)

DOOR

ROUGH SURFACE

Another common shortcut is to skimp on the use of sandpaper. Sanding takes time, but it's the difference between a good paint job and a poor paint job. Each coat of paint, stain, and sealer must be sanded and dusted before the next coat is applied. When this sanding process is omitted, the surface feels rough to the touch. The roughness can be bad enough to snag (or even hang) pantyhose. The last coat, however, should not be sanded.

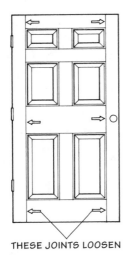

THESE JOINTS LOOSEN

Naturally, entry doors should operate smoothly. The joints of a sticky or binding door will eventually loosen, which will worsen the condition and even ruin the door. Steel doors are a good choice here, but they're not as good-looking as wood doors.

Check the hardware on interior doors. They should all have three hinges. Two hinges will work for a while, but three will keep a door hanging straight and swinging smoothly for years.

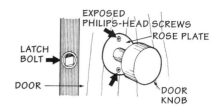

Check the lockset, too. Cheap locksets have their latch bolt housed in a simple cylinder. Their attachment screws are exposed, too. These locksets don't hold up well. The screws require frequent tightening, and the latch-bolt cylinder sometimes loosens.

Better locksets have latch-bolt front plates that are recessed and screwed into the edge of the door. Their screw-fastening systems are superior, and the screws are covered by an outside rose plate. The best locksets cost. Most companies offer different qualities. Don't go by brand name alone. You get what you pay for.

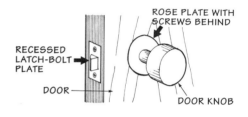

Check the latch-bolt front plate and the strike plate. A good craftsman will install them so they look as if they were cast in place.

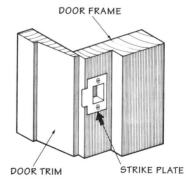

CHAPTER SEVENTY-THREE

Review with a "Roving Eye"

I always have a roving eye whenever I visit a house, new or old. I can tell pretty quickly if the builder knows his craft. So whenever I am called on to examine a house, I use the same technique—the roving eye.

I start by standing well away from the house to get an overall general impression. Most look great from this perspective, and many a house is purchased as a result of this view.

Then I move in close to check the quality of the work—first outside, then inside. This is where you can tell if you're getting a good house.

You can cultivate a roving eye, too. Here is what you should look for.

1. Ground should slope away from house, especially at window wells and ground-level doors.
2. Level entry steps with neat masonry work; no cracks.
3. Wood trim spaced off masonry.
4. Well-put-together wood trim; no splits or warps.
5. Neat siding job; no splits, warps, or missing shingles.
6. Three-coat paint job with nails set and filled.
7. Neat gutter installation, with proper slope toward downspouts.
8. Proper offset of joints on a wood-shingle roof.
9. A straight roof-shingle line along the gable ends from eave to ridge.
10. Straight shingle line along roof valleys.
11. A good grade of asphalt shingles.

12. Neat masonry work and good flashing on the chimney.
13. Neat concrete work on garage floor and apron; no cracks. A plus is a dropped apron with an angle iron at the drop.
14. A smoothly operating front door; no binding.
15. Floor free of squeaks and laid up tight, with proper joint stagger.
16. Baseboard trim hard against the floor; no gaps.
17. Good baseboard joints at corners and doors, well nailed with no splits.
18. Good joints in door and window trim, well nailed with a smooth finish.
19. Easily operating windows with no sticking.
20. Well-fitted doors showing an equal space all around between door and frames.
21. Three hinges on all doors and a good grade of hardware.
22. Neat installation of door hardware.
23. Smooth finish on all doors, stained or painted, with tops and bottoms painted or stained and sealed.
24. Neat drywall joints, no nail pops, and crack-free over doors and windows.
25. Bookshelves 3/4 inch thick spanning no more than 2 feet, 6 inches.
26. Neat joints at countertops with a good fit against the wall.
27. Good grade of cabinet hardware.
28. Neat, clean fireplace masonry work. Narrow mortar joints in brickwork look best.
29. Solid newel posts at stairways. Good joint where handrail meets newel post.
30. Nonsqueaking stairs.
31. Balusters set into handrail and tread, not toenailed.
32. Good joint where tread meets the wall trim (stringer).
33. Dry basement; no water stains on walls or floor.
34. Crack-free walls. Snap-tie holes filled.
35. Minimum number of floor cracks. They are almost impossible to avoid; one or two acceptable.
36. The main beam in the basement should be steel. If the main beam is wood, it must be of the flush type, not a dropped beam.

Index